8-15-50

Oh! Almighty and Everlasting
God, Creator of Heaven, Earth and the
Universe:—

Help me to be, to think, to act what
is right, because it is right; make
me truthful, honest and honorable
in all things; make me intellectually
honest for the sake of right and
honor and without thought of
reward to me. Give me the ability
to be charitable, forgiving and pa-
tient with my fellowmen — help me
to understand their motives and
their shortcomings — even as Thou
understandest mine!

Amen, Amen, Amen.

The prayer on this page has been said by me—by Harry S. Truman—from high school days, as window washer, bottle duster, floor scrubber in an Independence, Mo., drugstore, as a timekeeper on a railroad contract gang, as an employee of a newspaper, as a bank clerk, as a farmer riding a gang plow behind four horses and mules, as a fraternity official learning to say nothing at all if good could not be said of a man, as a public official judging the weaknesses and shortcomings of constituents, and as President of the United States of America. (Handwritten in pencil—dated 8/15/50)

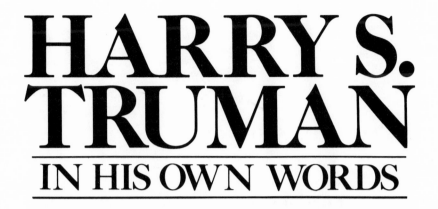

HARRY S. TRUMAN
IN HIS OWN WORDS

by William Hillman

Photographs by Alfred Wagg

BONANZA BOOKS
New York

This 1984 edition is published by Bonanza Books, distributed by Crown Publishers, Inc., by arrangement with Farrar, Straus, and Giroux, Inc.

Previously published as *Mr. President: The first publication from the personal diaries, private letters, papers and revealing interviews of Harry S. Truman.*

Manufactured in the United States of America

Library of Congress Cataloging in Publication Data

Truman, Harry S., 1884-1972.
    Harry S. Truman In His Own Words
    1. Truman, Harry S., 1884-1972.   2. United States — Politics and government — 1945-1953.   3. Presidents — United States — Biography.
I. Hillman, William, 1895-   .   II. Title.
E742.5.T62 1984   973.918′092′4   [B]   84-4218
ISBN 0-517-446367

h g f e d c b a

Contents

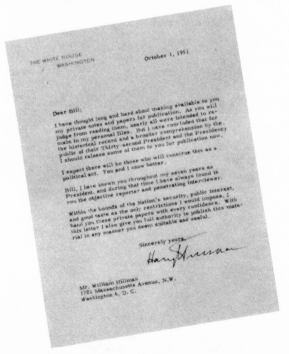

Foreword

PRESIDENT TRUMAN said to me: "I want the people to know the Presidency as I have experienced it and I want them to know me as I am."

This is the idea and the theme of this book.

I am a reporter.

This book began when Mr. Truman granted me a series of special interviews during which he discussed the basic policies of his administration against the background of his surprising and reflective knowledge of American and world history. As Mr. Truman answered my questions, a book of extraordinary significance emerged. The President made available to me all his diaries, his private papers and correspondence. With characteristic candor and directness, the President spoke out as no President ever has while in office.

History makes its judgments looking backward. Mistakes are corrected at leisure—retrospectively. Men and events that still endure in memory frequently look different to different generations.

The advent of communication with the speed of light, and the fierce insecurity of man, swiftly growing with his expanding knowledge, have generated a new force of spontaneous world opinion.

This force makes its own history: on the run, propelled by passions quickly touched and propaganda intruding as facts. Judgments are swift in the making and actions are quick to follow and too often the facts are slow to catch up. This new force of spontaneous world opinion has an enormous influence on the function and the leverage of the Presidency of the United States.

Never in history has any man been assigned the responsibilities the President has today.

Present-day human needs and still ancient human wants and ambitions, wherever men are, seem to be reaching out for attention by one man—whatever his constitutional limitations may be or however constructed he is in mind and spirit. There is no parallel for the world's intrusion today on the man in the White House. Hence, a close-up view of the President in action may prove useful to contemporary society. Since we are living in a kind of world where there is no precedent or parallel for some vital things, we cannot defer to the leisure of retrospective history what ought to be told now—even if only in part.

A world facing a perilous hour and even extinction would think it folly to allow academic or political considerations to obscure the President while he is in office. Certainly the

[1]

people of this country should welcome disclosure of a man they rarely meet—for that in effect is what most of the presidents of the United States have been to the American people. The man he would meet—while he is still in the White House—is what every American would like to know. The man as he really is is what every American would meet if he were able personally to call on the President in the White House and spend some time discussing the State of the Union and the State of the World.

No one understands this better than President Truman. That is why he is allowing me the unprecedented privilege of publishing some notes from his diary and his memoranda, while he is still in the White House.

The history of President Truman's administration and the final story of President Truman has yet to be written: first, because he is still in the White House, and second, because documents and materials affecting security and persons must for a time remain undisclosed and cannot be used. But the President, who hopes that history will remember him as a man of peace and who takes humble pride in being called by some of his friends "Mr. Democracy," has foregone personal consideration in permitting me to quote him directly about the basic aims of his administration; and especially to reveal his unrehearsed private thoughts as he set them down from time to time either in his diaries or his personal longhand written notes. The President tells me he has no intention of writing a book about himself, although he hopes that when he leaves the White House he may lecture on the problems of government under the general title of "From Precinct Worker to President."

The President thought it best to limit the publishing of any material from his diaries up to the end of 1949—in order to meet any charge that the writer had biased his material and had been merely selective. This action partially provides the safety of not publishing anything so contemporaneous as to be damaging to anyone domestic or foreign. It leaves interesting and vital historic data for publication at a more propitious time. However, in order to provide more comprehensive perspective in the presentation of the conduct of the President and the Presidency, it has been necessary to supplement the diary with direct exposition of his views on major events and his thinking, covering the period from the end of 1949 to date, as well as from April 12, 1945, when he became President, in those instances where he did not deem it proper to quote either from the diaries or memoranda.

The reading of the complete diaries and personal notes reveals a man sure of his purpose and so sure in his knowledge of history, that he stands steadfast in the stream of today's events, surefooted and with a deep sense of his responsibilities, acting with deliberation, often prophetic in his judgments.

This then is a book about and of President Truman in the White House. It is a book about the President as a person; a man of surprising knowledge and range of interests; of simple tastes and fierce convictions and opinions and old-fashioned sentiments and forward-looking social liberalism; about his almost slavelike devotion to duty and hard work; about his loneliness, a loneliness that is the fate of all presidents.

For a President walks pretty much alone—and never more so than when he is openly facing the crowd or dealing with the tangled problems of the country. He is most dramatic as he moves from decisions that shape the destiny of men around the world to the trivialities that are an essential part of everyday life in the routine of a President.

Conscious deeply of the spontaneous world opinion that makes its own history today President Truman, thumbing through some history books like the professor he hopes to be some day, told me: "You know, if Andrew Johnson, for example, had *not* given special interviews to a number of different newspaper correspondents, voicing his views on problems confronting him, a good deal of important historic material of the Presidency of Andrew Johnson might not have been unearthed or even known.

"I hope, in making some things plain to you at this time, especially in what I might say that affects me as a person, apart from the role of the President—which is all spread out on the official record—that perhaps the American people and the people of the world will understand a little better what I am trying to do and historians will have additional authentic data to what is disclosed by the archives. The notes you have seen were never intended for publication and are written in simple words and are not polished up. I hope they will serve the purpose of clarifying some things, just as they helped me to clarify my thinking as I wrote them."

I want to make one thing clear. The President himself had forgotten many of the handwritten memoranda which I found among his papers, turned over to me by his private secretary. Where they were used he requested that they not be changed nor edited in any way.

WILLIAM HILLMAN

Sept. 26, 1918 a few minutes before 4 A.M.

A serious man of my acquaintance was standing behind a battery of French 75's, at a little town called Neuville to the right of the piquage front. A barrage was to be fired by all the guns on the Allied front from Belgium to the Swiss border.

At 4 A.M. that barrage started at 5 A.M. the infantry in front of my acquaintance's battery went over. At 8 A.M. the artillery including the 75 battery

and the same old pacifists began to talk disarmament. But my acquaintance tried to meet every situation and has met them up to now. Can he continue to outface the demagogues, the chislers, the jealousies?

Time only will tell. The human animal and his emotions change not much from age to age. He must change now

PART ONE

Problems of the Presidency

I

Looking over the private papers of the President I came across a handwritten memorandum of eight pages on White House stationery. I almost missed the significance of it. It started with the sentence "Sept. 26, 1918, a few minutes before 4 A.M. a service man of my acquaintance . . ." I was eager to get into documents of more recent date and having more immediate and personal impact. However, I read on:

"Sept. 26, 1918, a few minutes before 4 A.M. a service man of my acquaintance was standing behind a battery of French 75's at a little town called Neuville to the right of the Argonne Forest. A barrage was to be fired by all the guns on the Allied front from Belgium to the Swiss border.

"At 4 A.M. that barrage started, at 5 A.M. the infantry in front of my acquaintance's battery went over. At 8 A.M. the artillery including the 75 battery moved forward. That forward movement did not stop until Nov. 11, 1918.

"My acquaintance came home, was banqueted and treated as returned soldiers are usually treated by the home people immediately after the tension of war is relieved.

"The home people forgot the war. Two years later, they turned out the administration which had successfully conducted our part of the war and turned the clock back.

"They began to talk of disarmament. They did disarm themselves to the point of helplessness. They became fat and rich, special privilege ran the country—ran it to a fall. In 1932 a great leader came forward and rescued the country from chaos and restored the confidence of the people in their government and their institutions.

"Then another European war came along. We tried as before to keep out of it. We refused to believe that we could get into it. The great leader warned the country of the possibility. He was vilified, smeared, misrepresented but kept his courage. As was inevitable

[7]

we were forced into the war. The country awoke—late, but it awoke and created the greatest war production program in history under the great leader.

"The country furnished Russia, Britain, China, Australia and all the Allies, guns, tanks, planes, food in unheard of quantities, built, manned and fought with the greatest navy in history, created the most powerful and efficient air force ever heard of, and equipped an army of 8½ million men and fought them on two fronts 12,000 miles apart and from 3,000 to 7,000 miles from the home base, and created the greatest merchant marine in history in order to maintain those two battle fronts.

"The collapse of the enemies of liberty came almost simultaneously, in May for the eastern front and in August for the western front.

"Unfortunately, the great leader who had taken the nation through the peace-time and war-time emergencies passed to his great reward just one month before the German surrender. What a pity for this to happen after twelve long years of the hardest kind of work; three and a half of them in the most terrible of all wars.

"My acquaintance who commanded the 75 battery on Sept. 26, 1918 took over.

"The same elation filled the home people as filled them after the first world war. They were happy to have the fighting stop and to quit worrying about their sons and daughters in the armed forces.

"Then the reaction set in. Selfishness, greed, jealousy raised their ugly heads. No war-time incentive to keep them down. The same old pacifists began to talk disarmament. But my acquaintance tried to meet every situation and has met them up to now. Can he continue to outface the demagogues, the chiselers, and the jealousies?

"Time only will tell. The human animal and his emotions change not much from age to age. He must change now, or he faces absolute and complete destruction, and maybe the insect age, or an atmosphereless planet will succeed him.

"1946"

I looked at the date at the end of the memorandum. 1946. Harry S. Truman had been President of the United States for over a year. With the modesty that characterizes his actions and thinking and still baffles many people, the thirty-second President of the United States was looking at himself and the country, objectively and philosophically.

I asked President Truman if he had ever dreamed of being President of the United States, since that seemed to be the dream of every American boy.

He said:

"Never. No, never. I was never an egoist. But, as you know, I studied the lives of great men and famous women; and I found that the men and women who got to the top were

those who did the jobs they had in hand, with everything they had of energy and enthusiasm and hard work.

"I had no idea that the lightning would ever strike me, as it has.

"The Presidency of the United States is a terrible responsibility for one man. Luckily, the ten years I spent in the Senate gave me some idea and background of what to expect."

I asked him if he would talk about the problems of the Presidency, just what the President faces as a man.

He said:

"The President has an executive job that is almost fantastic. There has never been one like it. I think no absolute monarch has ever had such decisions to make or the responsibility that the President of the United States has. It is really fantastic. That may not be a good word to use in regard to the Presidency, but after all, every final important decision has to be made right here on the President's desk, and only the President can make it. Nobody else can do it for him, and his decisions affect millions not only in his own country but around the world. As you see, I need the best information and advice that I can get. I believe honest men will arrive at honest decisions if they have the facts."

I asked, "Can any one man alone today handle the work of the Presidency?"

He replied:

"No one man really can fill the Presidency. The Presidency has too many and too great responsibilities. All a man can do is to try to meet them. He must be able to judge men, delegate responsibility and back up those he trusts."

"And he must have courage?" I asked.

He said:

"Well, yes. But if a President knows what the implications are of any action he takes, he will be better able to act, and he will be forthright. You must know the historical background of what makes the world go round. After all, there is little real change in the problems of government from the beginnings of time down to the present. Those problems today are just about the same as they were for Mesopotamia and Egypt, for the Hittites, for Greece and Rome, for Carthage and Great Britain and France.

"The one great difference between the problems of governing in ancient and earlier days and today is that the people whom the ancients used to call "down below," the people who today exercise the real sovereignty, are better acquainted with what government means, and with what the purpose of government is.

"You know, government is an intangible thing. You hear people talk about the powers of the President. In the long run, his powers depend a good deal on his success in public relations. The President must try to get people to do the things that will be best for the most people in the country. I often say that I sit here at the President's desk talking to people and kissing them on both cheeks trying to get them to do what they ought to do without getting kissed.

"The President of the United States represents 154,000,000 people. Most of them have no lobby and no special representation. The President must represent all the people.

"Therefore, the President must be a sort of super-public relations man. His powers are great, but he must know how to make people get along together. The President spends a great deal of his time trying to make people get along together. His ceremonial duties which are incidental to his official duties are all part of his public relations duties.

"Some people think that public relations should be based on polls. That is nonsense.

"I wonder how far Moses would have gone if he had taken a poll in Egypt?

"What would Jesus Christ have preached if He had taken a poll in the land of Israel?

"Where would the Reformation have gone if Martin Luther had taken a poll?

"It isn't polls or public opinion alone of the moment that counts. It is right and wrong, and leadership—men with fortitude, honesty and a belief in the right that make epochs in the history of the world.

"Today the responsibility of the President is greater than ever. The President has to know what takes place all around the world. He has to have all sorts of world contacts. Because today we are, whether we like it or not, the most powerful nation in the world.

"I think this is the most remarkable Republic in the history of the world."

The President got up from his desk to point at a globe. He continued:

"This Republic has grown from a handful of colonies, right along here, with three million in population, to 154 million, with a national income of 272 billion dollars and a national production of 329 billion dollars. Those are the latest figures I have in the economic report right here.

"And it is amazing. Our appropriation for military business this year is greater than the national income of Great Britain. And so we have to assume the responsibility that we never thought we would have to assume, and which we tried to dodge for thirty years and which got us into another war. We just can't dodge that responsibility now.

"And the way to keep our economy on an even keel and keep it expanding is to encourage and help the development of the rest of the world.

"There will come a time when many of the things we need we will have to get from outside of the United States. We have to go to Labrador and to Liberia to get the ore necessary to keep our steel plants running. We have to go abroad for the copper we need. We

AT THE GLOBE IN THE EXECUTIVE OFFICE IN
THE WHITE HOUSE

have got copper in Arizona and Utah, but we can't get along without the copper of Chile. And there is tin in Bolivia and Malaya and rubber in Indonesia and, of course, I could add to the list of the things that we need from other parts of the world.

"As a matter of fact, we have got to interest ourselves in people of other countries, giving them a proper return for the production of the things we need, so that we can keep our own great production program going. That is the only way it can be kept going—it can't be done any other way. We can expand only if the world expands and that is why the President today has to know what is going on around the world and that is why he has greater responsibility. Because without knowing what is going on around the world he cannot exercise his judgment for his own country."

II

President Truman believes that the doctrine of the indispensable man is a danger to democracy.

He said:

"There is no indispensable man in a democracy. When a republic comes to a point where a man is indispensable, then we have a Caesar.

"I do not believe the fate of the nation should depend upon the life or health or welfare of any one man.

"When I became President I decided that the administrative side of the executive branch of the government should be so organized that not only would it function as well as possible at the present but that it would work efficiently for the future no matter who was at the head of the government.

"Our government is divided into three branches, the executive, the legislative and the judicial.

"I believe each branch has its own vital duties to perform.

"I do not believe the legislative branch should infringe on the duties of the executive and I have always resisted such infringement. I have been just as strong in my belief that the executive should not encroach on legislative functions.

"To be more effective as Chief Executive and administrator I had to reorganize the executive offices.

"You know, George Washington was the best administrator this country ever had, and I say this acknowledging that the scope and problems of government have increased hundred-fold since Washington's time.

"One of the hardest-working Presidents we ever had was Grover Cleveland. But Cleveland did not believe in delegating authority and for this reason had to slave away at his desk which was constantly piled up with mounds of paper.

"You see, I have stacks of paper here. But documents and reports that reach this desk have recommendations and suggestions attached to them by my cabinet members, or heads of federal agencies because I insist on having all the facts presented to me. To make sure that I get the facts I need, I also had to reorganize the office and staff of the President. A staff has been set up in the White House which consists of the press secretary, the assistant to the President, the secretary who makes appointments, the legal counselor, the personnel executive, the correspondence secretary and the aides representing the three defense services. The staff reports to me every morning and gets its instructions for the day.

"One of the basic things I did was to set up a Central Intelligence Agency. Admirals Leahy and Souers, and the State, Defense, Treasury and Commerce Departments all helped me to set it up.

"Strange as it may seem, the President up to that time was not completely informed as to what was taking place in the world. Messages that came to the different departments of the executive branch often were not relayed to him because some official did not think it was necessary to inform the President. The President did not see many useful cables and telegrams that came from different American representatives abroad.

"I decided to put an end to this state of affairs.

"The Central Intelligence Agency now co-ordinates all the information that is available to the State Department, the Department of Defense, and the individual offices of the Army, Navy and Air Force, the Department of Commerce, and the Treasury. In this way I am able to get a concentrated survey of everything that takes place. If I need any elaboration I ask for it. I get a report from the Central Intelligence Agency every morning. In cases of emergency I got special reports. I get special reports on the situation in Korea throughout the day. I get a special report every day from the Secretary of State covering the entire diplomatic field. And once a week the director of the Central Intelligence Agency comes to see me and makes a personal report. He usually brings me a report in this form."

The President took from his desk a large loose-leaf black book, but without opening it he promptly returned the book to the desk.

He continued:

"The report contains a complete roundup of all the military, diplomatic and economic news—a digest of all the cables that have come in during the week, especially the important ones, although I may have seen them before. In this way I am able to get all the facts in relation to one another."

THE PRESIDENT HOLDS HIS MORNING STAFF MEETING

I said to the President: "Certainly this seems to have been an important step."

He said:

"It was never done before. The President up to that time had to make decisions sometimes 'by guess and by God,' which is not a very satisfactory way to do business."

The President fondly calls the Central Intelligence Agency the "cloak and dagger" boys, and is very proud of the work being done by this new agency.

But the reorganization of the executive office did not stop there.

President Truman went on:

"An administrator cannot run the whole show himself, no matter what the institution is, government or business.

"He must have an efficiently organized staff around him and then he must delegate authority."

I asked: "In what way do you delegate authority?"

He said:

"The duty that you expect a fellow to carry out is specifically outlined, and he is given the authority to carry it out, and if he carries it out in a proper manner, he is backed to the limit by the President. This doesn't mean that he abdicates any power, because it is also made clear that proper reports will be made to him and that he will be consulted on major decisions, just as for example Charles Wilson meets with me at least once a week. Once a week I meet with the Secretary of Defense, who has as much authority as nearly any other man in the Government, and we discuss fundamental basic questions. The same with the other cabinet officers as the state of the union requires. Once a week and sometimes twice a week I meet with the Cabinet.

"When a fellow is given a job, he is directed to carry out that job, and if he does it as he should, he is backed to the limit by the President, and that constitutes a delegation of authority."

I asked how he had organized his personal staff.

He explained:

"I inherited some excellent men from Roosevelt's staff. But I expanded the staff and set up a personnel office in the White House which relieved me individually of conducting endless interviews.

"Then I went ahead with my reorganization by setting out for each assistant a certain kind of work to do, and each confines himself to that task. Naturally the executive assistants consult together, just as any other staff would and in that way it saves me from having to make trivial decisions."

One of the most trying responsibilities of the President must be the judging of men.

I asked the President how he judged men, if he had any rule of thumb by which he selected men for different jobs.

Mr. Truman said:

"You have got to have a pretty good picture of the background and history of men, and what their connections have been, both in business and personal life. And then you have just got to be a judge of people. I am not very often mistaken in judgments I make of

WITH JOSEPH H. SHORT, PRESIDENTIAL PRESS SECRETARY

people, because I think I understand people pretty well. But you always take a chance when you put a fellow in a position of responsibility, because no matter how good he is you cannot tell what he will do until he is tried.

"There are disappointments but they are fewer than you would think. It is the job of any administrator to know how to judge men, I don't care whether he works in a packing house, a newspaper, or a bank or in government—it's all the same."

I then asked the President about his Cabinet. The Cabinet in recent administrations had fallen into a sort of rubber-stamp pattern.

Mr. Truman said:

"I think I have revived the cabinet system and that I have made it work as a real group of administrators and advisers to the President.

"I set the Cabinet up on the same basis that my staff is set up. Each cabinet officer tends to his own business. If he has any suggestions to make to another cabinet officer, he makes them to that cabinet officer at a cabinet meeting, and if it is a matter that needs to be discussed at a cabinet meeting, it is nailed down there and everybody knows what is going on.

"At least once a week and sometimes twice a week I have cabinet meetings and discuss what affects each department, so that all the other departments know what is going on. That way, there is always good feeling between members of the Cabinet. I think I have got the most cooperative Cabinet that any President ever had. There is no clash in my Cabinet at the present time at all. If there is I'll soon see that something is done about it.

"One thing I should like to make clear. I always consult with my Cabinet on major policy decisions. It is much better having pooled brains on important subjects than trying to have one head do the work."

I asked him a blunt question as to whether the itch for power, or "Potomac fever," as the President calls it, had not given him some trouble from the men around him.

Mr. Truman answered frankly:

"Yes, I have had some men around here with the itch for power or self-aggrandizement. Maybe they go together. I have had two or three cabinet members and executive assistants who have gotten big heads.

"But, after all you know I have had more cabinet officers than most any other President and I have had less trouble with them than many Presidents. I like people. I still trust people, because I believe the majority of them can be trusted."

"Many Presidents have had what is known as 'palace intrigue' or 'palace bickering.' You always find that there is an excellent chance for jealousy and bickering among people who are close to the fount of power. You have to watch that all the time. Most of the times I

WITH MAJOR GENERAL WALLACE GRAHAM, PRESIDENTIAL PHYSICIAN

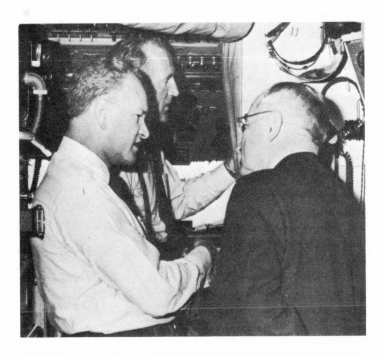

WITH HIS AIR AIDE MAJOR GENERAL ROBERT B. LANDRY
AND HIS PILOT COLONEL FRANCIS W. WILLIAMS

have had to make changes in the official family around the White House is when someone gets too big for his breeches, or he makes it unpleasant for those that he has to serve."

I pointed out that he had had four secretaries of state, and that many people believed the foreign policy changed with each new Secretary of State.

He said:

"Yes, I have had four secretaries of state, of course—but there has been no basic change in the foreign policy as I have laid it down. That foreign policy is based on this country's desire and my own wish to keep the peace of the world, if we can.

"I have had several secretaries of commerce and secretaries of labor but the fundamental lines of policy have not deviated from those laid down by the President.

"But I want to repeat. The ability to get the facts is one of the President's greatest problems. He cannot operate without trusting people. And I do trust people. There are ever so many more good men than bad ones in the world.

"I like to have people understand each other, and that is why I have every shade of public opinion in my Cabinet.

"I have got a cross section of the thought and economics of the whole population of the United States in the Cabinet from left to right. And this makes for valuable discussions, and the only way you can get ideas. And I let everybody have his say before I come to a conclusion and decide on a final course of action."

At this point I called the attention of the President to a memorandum-letter he had among his papers addressed to James F. Byrnes, Secretary of State, and written January 5, 1946.

This memorandum-letter is important for two reasons.

It makes clear the President's practice of delegating authority. But also he always insists on making the final decision in all policy matters.

And for the first time it reveals President Truman's very early and clear-cut estimate of the Russian situation and his determination to deal with it in realistic and vigorous terms.

The President, in permitting me to make this private memorandum or letter public, cautioned that I keep in mind that many events had occurred since this memorandum, notably the completion of a peace treaty and a defensive arrangement between the United States and Japan.

The President took this occasion to emphasize his and this nation's peaceful aims toward Russia, saying that Russia can have peace any time Russia really wants peace.

Here is the historic memorandum with note signed H.S.T. attached.

[*I wrote this memo and read it to my Secretary of State. So urgent were its contents I neither had it typed nor mailed but preferred to read it in order to give emphasis to the points I wanted to make. H.S.T.*]

January 5, 1946

"HON. JAS. F. BYRNES
SECRETARY OF STATE

"MY DEAR JIM: I have been considering some of our difficulties. As you know I would like to pursue a policy of delegating authority to the members of the Cabinet in their various fields and then back them up in the results. But in doing that and in carrying out that policy I do not intend to turn over the complete authority of the President nor to forego the President's prerogative to make the final decision.

"Therefore it is absolutely necessary that the President should be kept fully informed on what is taking place. This is vitally necessary when negotiations are taking place in a foreign capital, or even in another city than Washington. This procedure is necessary in domestic affairs and it is vital in foreign affairs. At San Francisco no agreements or compromises were ever agreed to without my approval. At London you were in constant touch with me and communication was established daily if necessary. That procedure did not take place at this last conference. I only saw you for a possible thirty minutes the night before you left after your interview with the Senate Committee.

"I received no communication from you directly while you were in Moscow. The only message I had from you came as a reply to one which I had Under Secretary Acheson send to you about my interview with the Senate Committee on Atomic Energy.

"The protocol was not submitted to me, nor was the communiqué. I was completely in the dark on the whole conference until I requested you to come to the Williamsburg and inform me. The communiqué was released before I ever saw it.

"Now I have infinite confidence in you and in your ability but there should be a complete understanding between us on procedure. Hence this memorandum.

"For the first time I read the Etheridge letter this morning. It is full of information on authority of the President nor to forego the President's prerogative to make the final decision.

Therefore it is absolutely necessary that the President should be kept fully informed on what is taking place. This is vitally necessary when negotiations are taking place in a foreign capital, or even in another city than Washington. This procedure is necessary in domestic affairs and it is vital in

maintain complete control of Japan and the Pacific. We should rehabilitate China and create a strong central government there. We should do the same for Korea.

Then we should insist on the return of our ships from Russia and force a settlement of their Lend Lease Debt of Russia.

I'm tired babying the Soviets

Sincerely

Harry S Truman

Rumania and Bulgaria and confirms our previous information on those two police states. I am not going to agree to the recognition of those governments unless they are radically changed.

"I think we ought to protest with all the vigor of which we are capable against the Russian program in Iran. There is no justification for it. It is a parallel to the program of Russia in Latvia, Estonia and Lithuania. It is also in line with the high-handed and arbitrary manner in which Russia acted in Poland.

"At Potsdam we were faced with an accomplished fact and were by circumstances almost forced to agree to Russian occupation of Eastern Poland and the occupation of that part of Germany east of the Oder River by Poland. It was a high-handed outrage.

"At the time we were anxious for Russian entry into the Japanese War. Of course we found later that we didn't need Russia there and that the Russians have been a headache to us ever since.

"When you went to Moscow you were faced with another accomplished fact in Iran. Another outrage if ever I saw one.

"Iran was our ally in the war. Iran was Russia's ally in the war. Iran agreed to the free passage of arms, ammunition and other supplies running into millions of tons across her territory from the Persian Gulf to the Caspian Sea. Without these supplies furnished by the United States, Russia would have been ignominiously defeated. Yet now Russia stirs up rebellion and keeps troops on the soil of her friend and ally—Iran.

"There isn't a doubt in my mind that Russia intends an invasion of Turkey and the seizure of the Black Sea Straits to the Mediterranean. Unless Russia is faced with an iron fist and strong language another war is in the making. Only one language do they understand—'How many divisions have you?'

"I do not think we should play compromise any longer. We should refuse to recognize Rumania and Bulgaria until they comply with our requirements; we should let our position on Iran be known in no uncertain terms and we should continue to insist on the internationalization of the Kiel Canal, the Rhine-Danube waterway and the Black Sea Straits and we should maintain complete control of Japan and the Pacific. We should rehabilitate China and create a strong central agreement there. We should do the same for Korea.

"Then we should insist on the return of our ships from Russia and force a settlement of the Lend-Lease debt of Russia.

"I'm tired babying the Soviets."

Turning back to a point the President had made earlier, I said:

"You believe in making people get together and in understanding one another, and you say they understand you as your Cabinet does. But don't you find that at first most of the average people who are not politicians are very shy or even frightened when they are introduced to you?"

Mr. Truman, speaking very slowly, said:

"When I do find people are frightened I always do everything I can to put them at ease. There is something awesome about the head of the United States—not me, but the Presidency itself—that causes people to become disturbed and rattled when they are around him.

I just have to think back to my first interview with President Roosevelt and I know exactly how they feel."

"When was your first interview with him?" I asked.

"Well, the first thing I did when I came down here as a Senator was to call on him and pay my respects and to tell him that I had been elected on his platform of 1932 and that I expected to support him. He was as cordial and nice to me as he could be. He always made you feel at ease after you had talked to him a little while.

"It was quite an event for a country boy to go calling on the President of the United States.

"And I always have to think back to that and understand so well how people feel when they come to see me.

"It would be a terrible thing for the President in his office to seem discourteous through lack of warmth to people who come to see him, because it hurts, and people never get over being hurt.

"I try my best to remember that all the time."

WITH MODEL OF STATUE OF ANDREW JACKSON

III

The President said the administrative reorganization of his office included a more thorough handling and consideration of bills sent him by Congress for approval or veto. He said: "In previous years a bill sent the President for action was submitted by the President's office for study and recommendation to the department of the government involved. I have all bills reviewed by most of the major departments since there might be implications affecting other fields that would otherwise be overlooked."

The President asked Mr. William J. Hopkins, Executive Clerk of the White House, to prepare a memorandum on how bills are sent to the President and how they are enacted into law or vetoed. Here is the memorandum:

Article I, Section 7, of the Constitution of the United States provides in part as follows:

"Every Bill which shall have passed the House of Representatives and the Senate shall, before it becomes a Law, be presented to the President of the United States; if he approve, he shall sign it, but if not, he shall return it, with his Objections to that House in which it shall have originated, who shall enter the Objections at large on their Journal, and proceed to reconsider it. If after such Reconsideration two-thirds of that House shall agree to pass the Bill, it shall be sent, together with the Objections, to the other House, by which it shall likewise be reconsidered; and if approved by two-thirds of that House it shall become a Law. But in all such cases the votes of both Houses shall be determined by Yeas and Nays, and the names of the persons voting for and against the Bill shall be entered on the Journal of each House respectively. If any Bill shall not be returned by the President within ten Days (Sundays excepted) after it shall have been presented to him, the Same shall be a Law in like Manner as if he had signed it, unless the Congress by their Adjournment prevent its Return; in which Case it shall not be a Law."

All Senate and House Joint Resolutions must be presented to the President for approval before they become law. But simple Resolutions of the Senate and House and Concurrent Resolutions of the Senate and House do not require the approval of the President.

Congressional action on a Bill or Joint Resolution having been completed, the enrolled enactment is signed by the presiding officer of both Houses and certified by the Secretary of the Senate or Clerk of the House, as the case may be. The enrolled enactment is then transmitted by hand to the White House by the appropriate official of the House in which the Bill originated. If the Bill originated in the Senate, an official of the Senate brings the enrolled enactment to the White House Office. If the Bill originated in the House, an of-

Washington 25, D. C.

OC̅ 2 3 195'

Honorable Frederick J. Lawton
Director, Bureau of the Budget
Washington, D. C.

Dear Mr. Lawton:

Reference is made to the transmittal under date of October
19, 1951, from the Assistant Director, Legislative Reference, Bureau
of the Budget, for the attention of the General Counsel of the General
Services Administration, of facsimile of enrolled bill (S. 921) entitled "An Act To amend section 304 of the Federal Property and Administrative Services Act of 1949 and section 4 of the Armed Services
Procurement Act of 1947".

Under this enrolled enactment section 304 of the Federal
Property and Administrative Services Act of 1949 and section 4 of the
Armed Services Procurement Act of 1947 would be amended by the
insertion at the end of each section of a new subsection (c). This
subsection would require that all contracts negotiated without advertising shall include a clause to the effect that the Comptroller
General of the United States or any of his duly authorized representatives shall, until the expiration of three years after final payment,
have access to, and the right to examine any directly pertinent books,
documents, papers, and records of the contractor or any of his subcontractors engaged in the performance of and involving transactions
related to such contracts or subcontracts.

The General Services Administration recommends Presidential
approval of S. 921.

Sincerely yours,

RUSSELL FORBES
Acting Administrator

RECEIVED
Oct 23 3 16 PM '51
BUREAU OF THE BUDGET

October 23, 1951

Honorable Frederick J. Lawton
Director, Bureau of the Budget
Washington, D. C.

My dear Mr. Lawton:

In compliance with Mr. Jones' request I have had examined
a facsimile of the enrolled bill (S. 921) "To amend section 304 of
the Federal Property and Administrative Services Act of 1949 and
section 4 of the Armed Services Procurement Act of 1947."

The bill would provide that all contracts negotiated without advertising pursuant to authority contained in the named Acts
shall include a clause giving the Comptroller General of the United
States access to the books and records of the contractors and subcontractors for a period of three years following final payment
under such contracts.

The Department of Justice perceives no objection to the
approval of the bill by the President.

Sincerely,

A. Devitt Vanech
Deputy Attorney General

RECEIVED
OCT 25 '5P DM '51
BUREAU OF THE BUDGET

OCT 26 1951

Dear Mr. Lawton:

Reference is made to the request by your office of October
19, 1951, for the views of this Department with respect to
S. 921, an enrolled bill "To amend section 304 of the Federal
Property and Administrative Services Act of 1949 and section 4
of the Armed Services Procurement Act of 1947".

That enrolled enactment would provide, with respect to the
Federal Property and Administrative Services Act of 1949, and the
Armed Services Procurement Act of 1947, that:

"All contracts negotiated without advertising pursuant to authority contained in this Act shall include
a clause to the effect that the Comptroller General of
the United States or any of his duly authorized representatives shall until the expiration of three years after
final payment have access to and the right to examine
any directly pertinent books, documents, papers, and
records of the contractor or any of his subcontractors
engaged in the performance of and involving transactions
related to such contracts or subcontracts."

As you know, this Department originally opposed this bill
because of the anticipated difficulties affecting the current
procurement program of the Department of Defense that would arise
as a result of its enactment. After telephone conversations with
representatives of your office and with certain Congressmen, this
office withdrew that original report and submitted a revised
report concurring with the favorable comments of the Bureau of
the Budget with respect to it.

Subsequently, this Department, with the consent of the
Bureau of the Budget, offered an amendment to the bill which
would have permitted an agency head, in cases where he deemed it
necessary to effect a procurement, to omit such a clause in contracts for supplies or services outside of the continental limits
of the United States, its territories, and possessions. That
proposed amendment was prompted by our apprehensions that the
indiscriminate inclusion of such a clause might jeopardize our
procurement program in foreign countries. Although the Congress

---

B-101404   October 22, 1951

Honorable Frederick J. Lawton, Director
Bureau of the Budget

My dear Mr. Lawton:

There has been received communication dated October 19, 1951, from
the Assistant Director, Legislative Reference, Bureau of the Budget,
enclosing a facsimile of enrolled enactment S. 921 entitled "AN ACT To
amend section 304 of the Federal Property and Administrative Services
Act of 1949 and section 4 of the Armed Services Procurement Act of 1947",
and requesting my comments thereon.

The Armed Services Procurement Act of 1947 and the Federal Property
and Administrative Services Act of 1949, as amended, are permanent legislation which provide the basic authority for a large part of the procure-
ments made by the Government, both for civilian and military purposes.
These laws authorize the negotiation of contracts without advertising on
determinations by the head of the department or agency concerned when
(1) a national emergency has been declared by the President or by the
Congress and (2) in a number of other specific circumstances, even though
a national emergency may not exist. As a matter of necessity the authority
to negotiate contracts has been delegated to a great many officers and
employees.

The provisions of S. 921 would add to the Armed Services Procurement
Act and the Federal Property and Administrative Services Act provision
for an independent examination by the General Accounting Office of the
underlying facts and costs of the performance of contracts and subcontracts
negotiated without advertising.

While I agree that in times of national emergency, and under other
particular circumstances, the authority to negotiate contracts is necessary,
I believe it absolutely essential that the use of this broad authority be
coupled with safeguards designed to bring to light any abuses of the
authority. The enactment of the provisions of S. 921 will greatly assist
in accomplishing this objective.

In administering the provisions of S. 921 it is not contemplated that
the General Accounting Office will make a detailed examination of the
books and records of every contractor or subcontractor holding a negotiated

ficial of the House of Representatives brings the enrolled enactment to the White House Office. The Bill is delivered to the White House Record Office, where it is signed for by number and the time of receipt indicated in the receipt book. A White House stamp indicating the day of its receipt at the White House is then placed on the left-hand margin of the Bill in the Record Office. The Constitutional ten days commences to toll on the first day (Sundays excepted) following the receipt of the Bill.

The Bills are then immediately sent from the Record Office to the Executive Clerk for custody and, by direction of the President, he promptly notifies the Director of the Bureau of the Budget in writing of the receipt of the Bills, and asks the Director to let the President have reports and recommendations as soon as possible. The enrolled enactment is retained in the custody of the White House Office.

It is the duty of the Bureau of the Budget to notify the appropriate Departments and Agencies of the President's desire to have the benefit of their reports and recommendations as soon as possible. The Bureau of the Budget and the Departments and Agencies work from facsimile copies of the enrolled enactment. On the receipt of these reports and recommendations, the Bureau of the Budget analyzes and co-ordinates them. In a covering letter transmitting these papers to the President, the Bureau digests the various recommendations and submits a recommendation of its own. In addition, the file contains a copy of the Bill as introduced, the Senate and House Reports, and a facsimile copy of the enrolled enactment. This process of co-ordination by the Bureau of the Budget may take anywhere from a matter of hours to a great portion of the ten days, depending upon the circumstances and the complexities of the Bill.

On receipt at the White House Office, these reports and recommendations are subject to such further analysis and study as the President may direct. When this study and analysis has been completed, the enrolled Bill is attached to the file and is ready for submission to the President for his official action.

This is the customary procedure. It may be modified by Presidential direction.

Should the President decide to approve the Bill, it is customary for him to do so by signing it to the left and below the signatures of the presiding officers of the Senate and the House. By hand stamp he also inserts the word "Approved" and the date above his signature. The Bill, together with the reports, is then returned to the office of the Executive Clerk for appropriate handling. The Bill itself, after proper recordation of the action of the President, is transmitted as promptly as possible to the General Services Administration to become a part of the permanent records of the Government in the National Archives. On delivery from the White House Office, a receipt is taken from the appropriate officials of the National Archives. The reports and recommendations are retained in the White House for the files of the President.

Should the President veto the Bill, he indicates no action at all on the enrolled enact-

Eighty-second Congress of the United States of America

AT THE FIRST SESSION

Begun and held at the City of Washington on Wednesday, the third day of January,
one thousand nine hundred and fifty-one

An Act

To amend section 304 of the Federal Property and Administrative Services Act of
1949 and section 4 of the Armed Services Procurement Act of 1947.

*Be it enacted by the Senate and House of Representatives of the
United States of America in Congress assembled,* That section 304 of
the Federal Property and Administrative Services Act of 1949 and
section 4 of the Armed Services Procurement Act of 1947 are hereby
amended by inserting at the end of the above-named sections the
following new subsection:

"(c) All contracts negotiated without advertising pursuant to
authority contained in this Act shall include a clause to the effect that
the Comptroller General of the United States or any of his duly authorized representatives shall until the expiration of three years after final
payment have access to and the right to examine any directly pertinent
books, documents, papers, and records of the contractor or any of his
subcontractors engaged in the performance of and involving transactions related to such contracts or subcontracts."

Speaker of the House of Representatives.

APPROVED

OCT 31 1951

Vice President of the United States and
President of the Senate.

ment but instead prepares a veto message returning the Bill to the House in which it originated with his reasons therefor. The Bill with the President's message is placed in a manila envelope addressed to the presiding officer of the appropriate House, sealed with a wax impression of the President's seal, and hand delivered by the Assistant Executive Clerk on the Floor while the House or Senate, as the case may be, is in session.

Should the President decide to let a Bill become Law without his approval, the enrolled enactment, after the expiration of ten days, is deposited with the National Archives for the permanent record of the Government. No notation is made on the Bill by the President, but a suitable memorandum accompanies it to the National Archives from the White House Office.

Should the Bill be pocket-vetoed by the President (allow ten days to expire after receipt of the Bill without taking action, the Congress having adjourned), it is customary for the President to sign a memorandum of disapproval, indicating the reasons for his action. There is no notation by the President on the enrolled Bill itself. The enrolled Bill and the President's Memorandum of Disapproval are retained in the White House Office.

IV

President Truman probably has written more letters than any other President of the United States, including Theodore Roosevelt. He likes to write letters. They provide a means of expression for his directness and friendliness. In spite of the terrific pressure of his daily schedule and the duties of office, he writes many personal letters a day, some in longhand, of which he seldom keeps copies, and others that are dictated.

The President said:

"I rarely write angry letters. As a matter of fact, aside from official letters, most of the letters I write are the letters of a good neighbor. I like to gossip with friends. I like to exchange views and opinion with people in all walks of life."

Here are some that are typical:

Margaret Ann Kurt, thirteen-year-old niece of Miss Rose Conway, the President's confidential secretary, had written thanking Mr. Truman for her first plane ride—on the presidential plane "Independence."

The President replied:

"I am so happy that you enjoyed your first plane ride. My first one was in France in 1918 and I had to do what I was ordered to do. It was in an old 'Jenny' and the pilot didn't want me to ride with him any more than I wanted to take the ride. I became very sick, due to all the gyrations he gave the plane.

"I was sick for many years after that whenever I took a flight in a plane. But I got over that. I'm glad you had a good start in flying. The Independence is tops."

Reminiscing again about his past, the President writes a friend, David M. Noyes:

"Bess and I have just returned from the station where we met our baby. She remarked that she felt as if she had been somewhere when both of us were on hand to meet her.

"When I came over to my Blair-Lee House office, I found your letter of September 26th about the bouquet that I ordered sent to you in the hospital.

"That letter made me very happy, not only because of the report on the doctors and the nurses and their feeling toward me but more important to me your 'I am now fully recovered.' I am so glad. . . .

"The date of your letter, September 26, brings some memories to me. On September 26, 1917, I went to Camp Doniphan at Ft. Sill, Oklahoma, to train (that's not the word) for service as a first lieutenant of field artillery. The colonel made me canteen officer of the regiment. I collected $2.00 a man from each battery, $2200.00 in all and set up a business. In six months I paid the money back to the various organization funds and $15,000.00 in dividends.

"They gave me a promotion and sent me to a special school in France. I went over on the George Washington with some 7000 other soldiers and landed in Brest on April 13, 1918. Went on to Montigny-sur-Aube and had Dick 'By God' Burleson for my teacher. He is an uncle of Jake Vardaman and some character. I sent him to Russia with Ed Pauley and he outcussed them all.

"On Sept. 26, 1918, I stood behind my battery and fired 3000 rounds of 75 shells from 4 A.M. to 7 A.M. and then went forward for more trouble than I was ever in before—but not *since*.

"Take good care of yourself, come to see me when you can and be very careful about writing a sentimental old man a sentimental letter—this is what you get!"

Both the above letters were written in longhand and were given me by the recipients.

———

Here is a dictated letter to Judge Harold R. Medina, dated June 19, 1951.

"I appreciate very much your letter of the fourteenth.

"You are certainly very lucky to have your mother with you at ninety-three. Mine lived to be ninety-four, and I am sure that if she hadn't fallen and broken her hip for the third time, she would have lived to be one hundred.

"I am very sure you will fill the place, left vacant by Judge Learned Hand, with credit and honor, as you have filled the District Court position in that manner.

"I was glad to have your analysis of what the little guys have to say. When you get right down to it they really are the backbone of the country and they are not so little either, as you stated in your communication."

————

Here is an historic letter, written to a friend, on April 10, 1951, the day on which he signed the order relieving General MacArthur of his command.

"I reached a decision yesterday morning, after much consideration and consultation on the Commanding General in the Pacific. It will undoubtedly create a great furor but under the circumstances I could do nothing else and still be President of the United States. Even the Chiefs of Staff came to the conclusion that civilian control of the military was at stake and I didn't let it stay at stake very long."

————

A letter dictated October 19, 1951, to Congresswoman Edna F. Kelly says:

"I appreciated most highly your good letter of the seventeenth and, of course, I am always happy to have your views on any subject.

"Things happen in the world which we have to meet just as you have to meet conditions in your own district. We try to meet them as best we can. Sometimes I am not right sure that we do meet them in the right way, but when decisions have to be made it never helps to hesitate.

"I appreciate most highly your viewpoint on the issues expressed in your letter."

————

Dictated and dated August 28, 1951, the President writes a former state senator, the Honorable George F. Clayton of Hannibal, Missouri:

"DEAR GEORGE: I have just received two booklets called 'Old Trails Area of Missouri' and 'Old Settlement Playgrounds of Missouri.' They are excellent and I hope you will keep publishing booklets such as these.

"I have been President of the National Old Trails Road Association since nineteen twenty-four, furnished the means to erect all of the monuments across the country referred to in the Old Trails booklet and have been in every corner of the state referred to in 'Old Settlement Playgrounds.'

"Arizona gets out a booklet like the ones you are publishing, and so do several of the other states, and I am very glad to see Missourians let the world know what a grand old state it really is."

The President answering a woman who had been disappointed because her son had not been able to get a commission in the Navy writes:

"A long time ago I was refused entrance to both Annapolis and West Point because I couldn't see. Years after that I was instrumental in helping to organize a National Guard

battery—that was in 1905. When the First World War came along, due to the fact that I had done a lot of studying, I was made a first lieutenant in the 129th Field Artillery in Battery 'F.' I attended the Fort Sill, Oklahoma, School of Fire and several other special schools. Finally I became a battery commander and an instructor in the Field Artillery firing for the regiment and the brigade.

"After the first World War, I organized the first Reserve Officers Association in the United States and became its President. Luckily, or unluckily, I then got into a political career, and you know the result. So you tell that son of yours not to be discouraged because he can't get exactly what he wants now. The thing to do is to take the next best, make the most of it, and you never can tell what will happen."

———

A President of the United States receives more mail perhaps than any other person. In addition to official mail there are letters of praise and letters of criticism and there are letters asking for something to be done. Mr. Truman takes his role as direct representative of all the people seriously. He tries to answer as many letters as is humanly possible. The range of subjects he must cover is as wide as the world. William D. Hassett, an ex-newspaperman who has been secretary to President Roosevelt as well as to President Truman, helps to frame answers to certain official and semi-official letters.

But the President believes letter-writing is as important as seeing people and the President loves seeing people.

I asked Mr. Truman: "Have you always liked to write letters?"
"Yes."
"Even as a boy?"
"Yes. I have always had correspondence with the family ever since I can remember. Always had. In fact, I was always the clearing house for all the family, even when they weren't speaking to each other. They were speaking to me. I got them all to the point eventually where there was no ill-feeling between us. And that's a job with a Kentucky outfit. You know my four grandparents came from Kentucky."

———

Very few presidents have been free of controversy resulting from letters they have written.

Because one letter written by Mr. Truman has caused some controversy I am quoting this short extract from his personal notes that supplemented his diary. It is handwritten in ink.

December 9, 1950

"Margie held a concert here in D.C. on Dec. 5th. It was a good one. She was well accompanied by a young pianist named Allison whose father is a Baptist preacher in Augusta, Georgia. Young Allison played two pieces after the intermission, one of which was the great A flat Chopin Waltz, Opus 42. He did it as well as it could be done and I've heard Paderewski, Moritz Rosenthal and Josef Lhévinne play it.

"A frustrated critic on the Washington Post wrote a lousy review. The only thing, General Marshall said, he didn't criticize was the varnish on the piano. He put my baby as low as he could and he made the young accompanist look like a dub.

"It upset me and I wrote him what I thought of him. I told him he was lower than Mr. X and that was intended to be an insult worse than a reflection on his ancestry. I would never reflect on a man's mother because mothers are not to be attacked, although mine was.

"Well, I've had a grand time this day. I've been accused of putting my baby who is the apple of my eye in a bad position. I don't think that is so. She doesn't either—thank the Almighty."

The President feels that members of a President's family have a special handicap because they are exposed to an unrelenting light, one that does not so expose and limit the

EDITOR'S TABLE.

—Not long since the papers duly chronicled the fact that Mrs. Lincoln bought a shawl for $5,000 ; then that she purchased a set of ear-rings and pin for $3,000. Other various purchases have been announced within the year, amounting to over $7,000. Here are $15,000 spent by "our rosy empress" in one year. But this is not all. She is on the wing about two-thirds of her time—traveling in especial trains of cars, stopping at the most expensive hotels, figuring on a scale of Babylonian magnificence, all of which cannot be less than $5,000 more for the year. So the whole foots up $23,000. That is within $2,000 of all Lincoln's salary. "Disloyal" people want to know where this vulgar, poverty-stricken lawyer from Illinois gets all the money to allow his wife such princely extravagance. Think of the hundreds of thousands of widows and orphans—think of the acres of poor soldiers whose bones lie bleaching upon a hundred battle-fields, or whose maimed forms are suffering in hospitals and poor-houses, all the work of this man—and then over against all this woe, set his wife, frolicking and rolling in a merry luxury that rivals the splendor of an eastern harem. When Lincoln started for Washington, after his election, he was not worth money enough of his own to pay the expenses of his journey to the capital. No, not enough to pay the railroad fare from Springfield to Chicago. What mine of wealth has he found at Washington? Enquire of the pockets of the people! The poor people!

—A London and a Paris author are disputing as to which is the freest country, England or France. These disputants do not seem to comprehend the difference between English and French freedom. It is very great. England is the country of *right* more than of liberty. Everything there is weighed by the standard of *justice* or of right. Inflexible justice is the rule, and that wears all the marks of the widest liberty. But it has not always, certainly not necessarily, the soul of liberty. In France it is just the reverse. That is the country of *liberty* more

than of *right*. There is the smallest domination over opinion. Good or bad, if a man believes a thing, he is left to the peaceable enjoyment of it. There is little restraint upon his heart and brain. So unlike is what is denominated freedom in France and England. In this country the same difference exists between the East and the West. The West is more like France—complete freedom of opinion, and almost entire exemption from social despotism. How different the East! In New England, indeed, real liberty is not known. Public opinion is a most galling and relentless tyranny. Social despotism is more absolute than political despotism in Austria or Turkey. If the time ever comes, which is not impossible, when New England will constitute a government by itself, it will be the narrowest despotism on earth. Every individual man will be in a strait jacket. The Puritan's narrow soul will have put those of unorthodox opinion in the stocks.

—To the lady who writes to know the difference between an *enthusiast* and a *fanatic*, we take pleasure in saying that the simple enthusiast is a quiet and harmless being. He sees visions and dreams dreams of all sorts of coming impossibilities ; but he generally is content to enjoy his fond ideas in peaceable retirement. The fanatic is over restless and turbulent. He is a dreamer as well as the enthusiast ; but so far from contenting himself with his dreams, he is impatient to rage and riot abroad. He is a disturber of other mens' peace, and an enemy of the rest and good order of society. The enthusiast may merit our respect or our pity ; the fanatic almost always deserves a halter.

—A strong-minded woman who has visited Mr. Lincoln reports him as saying that he sighed for some soft pillow of rest from the turmoils of office. Montaigne says : "Ignorance is the softest pillow a man can lay his head upon." If that is so, we advise Mr. Lincoln to go to sleep at once, and sleep away the remainder of his ill-starred and pestilent

THE JEFFERSON MEMORIAL

ambitions and privacies of most men and women. There are frequent references in the President's diary to the hope that the fact he is President will not color or thwart the career of his daughter.

Thanking a newspaperman for sending him a booklet on Lincoln's re-election he wrote:

"As you know, Mrs. Lincoln was the most persecuted woman who ever lived in the White House and the article about her in the back of the booklet that you sent me, is a sample of what they did to her all over the country."

The President resents misuse of his letters even if they are turned as weapons against political opponents.

Senator Robert A. Taft of Ohio was criticized for having written a letter of congratulation to Mr. Truman in 1948 in which it was alleged Senator Taft expressed delight at Mr. Dewey's defeat. Senator Taft asked the President for a copy of his letter since it was a handwritten one. The President had his files searched. The Ohio Senator made public a copy of his own letter sent him by the President.

Mr. Truman's covering letter written October 17, 1951, said:

"DEAR BOB:

"I finally found the letter of congratulations which you wrote me on November 6, 1948, and I am enclosing you a copy of it. I appreciated it very much when I received it and I still think very highly of it and I am glad to send you a copy of it. It was written in longhand on board the Vulcania and evidently mailed when the ship arrived at port.

"I see you have thrown your hat in the ring and I suppose you will have all the fun that goes with that sort of decision."

Senator Taft's letter read:

November 6, 1948

MY DEAR MR. PRESIDENT:

"I wish to extend my hearty congratulations on your election, and I hope to do the same in person on my return to Washington about December 15. There are many matters on which we can agree to disagree. On the other hand there may be some others where I can be of help in eliminating unnecessary legislative difficulties.

"Mrs. Taft joins me in sending our best wishes for a happy four years to Mrs. Truman and yourself."

I asked the President for permission to use a letter which has been the source of much speculation and even controversy. It is a letter to Mr. Bernard Baruch, written before the 1948 campaign.

On August 19, 1948, the President wrote Mr. Baruch as follows:

"DEAR MR. BARUCH:

"I was talking with Senator McGrath yesterday and he suggested that it would be very greatly to the advantage of the Democratic organization if you would agree to serve on the Finance Committee. I hope you will be willing to do that.
    P.S. Congratulations on your birthday today."

Mr. Baruch replied he could not accept the invitation.

On August 31, 1948, the President replied:

"MY DEAR MR. BARUCH:

"I read your letter of the twenty-seventh with much disappointment. A great many honors have passed your way, both to you and your family, and it seems when the going is rough it is a one-way street. I am sorry that this is so.
    "P.S. I've appointed Mrs. William G. McAdoo and Mrs. Thos. J. Watson to be Special Representatives at the coronation of Princess Juliana, along with the Ambassador to the Netherlands."

The Ambassador to the Netherlands at that time was the Hon. Herman Baruch, brother of Barney Baruch.

The file of the President's letters, already greater than that of Franklin Delano Roosevelt, reveals not only a wide range of interest but a richness of historical and political detail.

Writing a friend, Mr. Truman said:

". . . my great-grandmother was a first cousin of Tyler. One of Tyler's father's brothers moved to Kentucky and my great-grandmother was his daughter. We never bragged about the fact though because none of the family thought much of old man Tyler as a President, although he did establish the precedent of making the Vice President, when he assumes office, actually the President of the United States and not acting President. His career as President was a peculiar one. He seemed to have no sense of proportion in his dealings with the Congress although he had had plenty of experience himself politically in coming up the ladder."

And again:

"There are certain people in this country, particularly those who have overnight become millionaires, that immediately become imbued with the idea that there ought to be a ruling class made up principally of those of great wealth, but that will never come to pass in this country.

"I have no prejudice with regard to the social and financial position of the people in this country. The thing I am principally interested in is to see that all parts of the population get a fair deal in the distribution of the resources of this great country of ours. I think we have made a magnificent success in that direction because the farmer, the work-

PRESIDENT JOHN TYLER

ingman and the business man's finances are in better condition than they ever have been in this country, or in the history of the world for that matter.

"I don't know why a man becomes greedy when he has everything he needs but it seems that the richer a man gets the more he wants when he would be much better off if he would spend his time trying to improve the wealth of other people after he attains success and sufficient money to see him through life. Some of them do but they're the exception and not the rule."

Again, in another letter:

"I have a complete review of the appointment of judges from the time of Teddy Roosevelt to the present and much to my surprise and to the surprise of the Republican organization, during the administrations of Theodore Roosevelt, William Howard Taft, Presidents Harding, Coolidge and Hoover there were not a half dozen Democrats appointed to the federal bench. President Roosevelt and myself have made more Republican appointments in proportion to the appointments than all those Republican Presidents put together."

Or, as practical a matter as this:

"I understand that there is a movement on foot to prevent the drawing of complete plans of the installations in the new White House. It is absolutely essential that the conduits, both wire and water, and all the complicated arrangements underneath the floors and the air conditioning service, be put on paper so that future mechanics of the White House can find things when it is necessary to make repairs. One of the difficulties with the old White House was that nobody knew where anything went and why it was there."

From the field of art and architecture:

"Not only would I like to see the Fine Arts Commission devote itself to building ornaments and paintings but I'd like very much to have a cultural start made in some of the key centers of the United States on the establishment of a real American culture. I've discussed this with several people and I hope you will be thinking about it and that you'll discuss it with any Ph.D.s and college professors who are interested in the subject."

Here is a typical forthright letter written in 1948 to a prominent distiller:

"Thanks very much for yours of the second, enclosing me a copy of a letter which you have written to Secretary Anderson.

"I've never been a 'dry'—never voted 'dry' in my life—but some of the antics of the distillers almost make me feel like doing just that and, I think, there are a lot of other people in the same frame of mind."

———————

As an example of varied interests, I picked the following letters from the private correspondence file of the President.

January 7, 1948

My dear Mr. Iturbi: I certainly appreciated the concert last night and was especially happy when you played the Chopin waltzes as an encore.

I am very fond of Chopin's music—in fact I have a number of records made by you of the very Chopin waltzes you played last night. I also have one of the Fantasie Impromptu and Polonaise in A flat. I have a Paderewski record of the Moonlight Sonata—it runs on both sides of three records and finally winds up with his Minuet.

"All my family and our guests were highly pleased with the program, as was I.

November 4, 1950

DEAR MRS. LHÉVINNE: Thanks very much for your good letter of October tenth, which has just now reached me. I don't know what the cause of the delay was.

I heard Mr. Lhévinne the first time in the early 1900s when he made one of his first tours of the United States. He stopped in Kansas City and I remember very distinctly that Paderewski, Moritz Rosenthal and Joseph Lhévinne all came within about three weeks of each other and each one of them played the famous A flat Opus 42 Chopin Waltz and played Blue Danube as an encore. That was when I made up my mind that Joseph Lhévinne was the greatest of them all. After that I heard him every time he came to town—I expect as much as half a dozen times. I think he had a touch and interpretation that has never been equaled. I have as many of his records as I have been able to obtain and I have almost worn out the Blue Danube I've played it so much.

I also have a Polonaise of Chopin's and I have the same Polonaise played by Iturbi. It is most interesting to compare the technique of the two men.

I certainly appreciate hearing from you, and I know that you are doing a great work at the Juilliard School of Music.

DEAR GRANDMA MOSES: I certainly appreciated your good letter of May twenty-third. I am glad you enjoyed your visit to Washington.

Mrs. Truman and I were delighted to see you at the dinner and to have you at the Blair House for tea. My piano playing doesn't amount to much but I am glad you enjoyed it.

I hope you have many, many happy years ahead of you.

July 24, 1951

DEAR MR. JUDSON: It is a most peculiar human trait how misinformation can travel.

For your information, I never played golf in my life, never had a golf club in my hands to tell the honest truth, except to look at it—so I couldn't possibly have fired a ball on the Independence Golf Course and hit anybody in the head.

The only time I went to the Independence Golf Course was for a picnic. I never played golf on the course in my life.

March 4, 1949

DEAR ERNIE: If I had had any Christmas cards you certainly would have received one but I quit sending Christmas cards when the number got up to three thousand some ten years ago.

I am glad you want to be on the Christmas card list and I am also glad you won the bet on the election. As Chief Justice Taft once said to Jay Lee, you are one of those rare birds who was right before Tuesday, November second.

———

February 1, 1949

Dear Mr. McIntyre: It was certainly kind and thoughtful of you to send me the picture of the U.S.S. Zeppelin on which I returned from France in 1919.

We left Brest on April the ninth and arrived in New York City on April twentieth, Easter Sunday morning.

For me it was a miserable passage because I am not a good sailor and the old Zeppelin rolled as far as possible without turning over—pitched frontward and reared backward like a Texas broncho would do. I spent most of my time in my bunk upon 'A' deck where the rolling and pitching was most heartily felt.

———

April 12, 1951

Dear Mr. Cavasin: I certainly appreciated the miniature brass model of the old 3.2. I had my first training as a field artilleryman way back early in the nineteen hundreds on a 3.2 cannon. When you fired the old thing it rolled back twenty yards and one of the orders in training was "cannoneers on the wheels" to roll it back into position.

Then they furnished us with a 3″ German piece which was used up to World War 1, and later we were equipped with the old French 75 mm with high wooden wheels. I commanded a battery of those old 75 mm and they were wonderful guns. Our new 105 mm are, in my opinion, one of the greatest field guns ever invented.

I can't tell you how very much I appreciate this old model cannon of days gone by with its rammer and everything that goes with it.

———

March 26, 1949

Dear Doctor Greenway: I appreciated very much your letter of the twenty-third, and I was particularly interested in your Masonic Research regarding the first President's career and my own. I did know that Andrew Jackson was a Grand Master of the Grand Lodge of Tennessee before he was elected President. I was Grand Master of the Grand Lodge of Missouri.

I am interested in historical data such as that to which you refer and I appreciate your informing me about your findings.

September 3, 1949

DEAR HARRY: I appreciated most highly your letter of the twenty-third and I know just what you are up against with preparing the Grand Master's address.

You inquire about the history of the gavel I am holding in the oil painting, which was presented to the Grand Lodge. That gavel is made from wood from an elm tree at Plainfield, Indiana, which was known as the Van Buren Elm. The tree fell down a year or two ago and the mayor was kind enough to have a gavel made for me from a part of it.

There is a story that Van Buren during his campaign for President got stuck in a mudhole at this point and had to get out in the mud and muss up his boots, which were highly shined. As a result of that a plank road was built from Plainfield to Indianapolis. A long time ago I had a gavel made from one of the planks from that road but it has become misplaced and I can't find it any more. When Woodrow Wilson was President the plank road was torn up and a concrete road put down in its place—I think that occurred along in 1915 or 1916.

I am doing everything I possibly can to be present on the morning of the twenty-ninth for the installation of Jim Bradford. It certainly is kind of you to ask me to come.

I know you have had a successful year as Grand Master and I want to congratulate you on it.

September 27, 1949

DEAR MR. MOORE: My cousin, Miss Nellie Noland, forwarded your letter of the twenty-third to me and I read it with a great deal of interest.

The bulwark of our free institutions, of course, is based on a public school system where every person, no matter what his station, may have access to education. Our public school system has been a shining success in this history of the Nation and I know it will continue to be just that.

One of the difficulties with all our institutions is the fact that we've emphasized the reward instead of the service. I can remember school teachers, both men and women, who received a stipend for their services but whose ideals consisted of teaching the rising generation that service is much more important than the reward for service. I fear very much that we haven't emphasized that fact enough, although our increasing population, increasing cost of living, and our insane idea of keeping up with the Joneses, has probably had its effect also on the public schools.

I've been trying to work out a federal system of help to education, particularly along material lines—that is improved buildings and increased salaries for teachers, but I think the fundamental purpose of our educational system is to instill a moral code in the rising

generation and create a citizenship which will be responsible for the welfare of the Nation. I do appreciate very much receiving your letter.

One day the President said that sometimes he wrote letters which he never sent but wished he had sent. For example, here is a letter written to a prominent journalist. The President had come to the conclusion, however, that it was "a waste of time to try to convince this particular gentleman."

This letter is so much a reflection of the President's thinking and style that I persuaded him to allow me to have the letter printed here:

It deals with the recently revised security rules of the government and the columnist had criticized the President for having listened to government officials trying to suppress news.

Sunday Oct. 1951

MY DEAR ——: I've just read your column about my security press conference. You give me credit for the responsibility of the men who were the sources of the information about which I talked. I wish that were true.

You see some of the generals and the admirals and the career men in government look upon the occupant of the White House as only a temporary nuisance who soon will be succeeded by another temporary occupant who won't find out what it is all about for a long time and then it will be too late to do anything about it.

You newspaper men have a complex that anyone who tells you of any of your many shortcomings is either ambitious to be a dictator or else he is an ignoramus. But you should take into consideration that we are no longer in the gay nineties of Ben Harrison, William McKinley or Teddy the Rough Rider.

We are faced with the most terrible responsibility that any nation ever faced. From Darius I's Persia, Alexander's Greece, Hadrian's Rome, Victoria's Britain, no nation or group of nations has had our responsibilities. If we could spend one year's military appropriations to develop the Euphrates Valley, the plateau of Ethiopia, the tableland of South America—if we could open the Rhine-Danube waterway, the Kiel Canal, the Black Sea Straits to free trade, if Russia would be a good neighbor and use her military expenditures for her own economic development, I would not have to scold the publishers for giving away our military secrets. Wish you'd do a little soul searching and see if at *great* intervals the President may be right.

The country is yours as well as mine. You find no trouble in *suppressing* news in which I'm interested. Why can't you do a little safety policing?

SOME OF THE PRESIDENT'S HONORARY DEGREES

V

As an illustration of the President's relations with certain public figures and his attitude on basic problems, I asked him for permission to publish the letters which follow.

September 7, 1945

JAMES FORRESTAL, SECRETARY OF THE NAVY:

Thanks a lot for yours of the fourth extending congratulations for yourself and Admiral King on the Japanese victory. I appreciate your letter very much but the people who really ought to be congratulated are the people like yourself, Admiral King and all those who worked with you and the other military and naval services—also those who worked on farms, in factories and everywhere else. I deserve no credit for the victory except the little I contributed as United States Senator. It was already won when I became President and all I had to do was carry out the program laid out and with the cooperation of such able people as yourself and your subordinates I was able to do it. We have a bigger job to do now.

September 24, 1945

Memorandum for: HONORABLE TOM CONNALLY:

Reported interview this morning in the *New York Times* and the *Washington Post* quotes me as saying that I will assume full responsibility for the policy on the Atomic Bomb. It is not an accurate statement. The statement made was that I would assume full responsibility for the recommendation to be made to the Congress on the policy. Of course, the policy will have to be finally determined by the Congress in the light of all available information. I consider it my duty to furnish the Congress with all the information I have available and suggest a policy to them for action.

———

In letters written to a friend, and to a Congressman, light is shed on a very important chapter of history.

September 19, 1945

We had three and one half million men in Europe and we were transferring two mil-

Discussing plans for
the campaign of 1944,
and many other things
of interest to the President
and the new nominee
for Vice President.
This was in July 1944.

H.S.T.

lion of those men to the Japanese front when that war suddenly ceased far ahead of the anticipated date.

We simply have to adjust ourselves to conditions as we find them. We are putting forth every effort possible to get the matter worked out fairly and equitably. I can't see why a straightforward statement of the facts, as they are, to your constituents wouldn't be the best way out. No man should be discharged except for length of service, and the other requirements. Men who have done the actual fighting should have priority.

September 12, 1945

The situation which has developed in Congress was expected by me and every effort has been made to expedite the return and demobilization of American soldiers and sailors. You must bear in mind that not even the most optimistic expected either the war in Europe, or the Japanese war, to end as suddenly as they did. A great deal of preparation had been made, anticipating the end of the Japanese war sometime in the early part of next year. All the necessary arrangements had been made for the redeployment of American troops for an attack on Japan in November. When millions of men from half a dozen armies are being moved from one side of the world to another, and plans suddenly have to be changed, it can't be done in one day.

I have asked Congress for patience and forbearance and, if they give it to me, I will get the job done as expeditiously as it is physically possible to get it done. Members of Congress are going to have to take the heat in order to keep an injustice from being done to the men who really did the fighting and to be sure that we know exactly where we are going when the demobilization takes place.

I am asking the members of Congress to do just as much thinking on this subject as I am doing and to at least leave the demagoguery out until next year. I know the majority of them are going to do just that, but some of them aren't.

———————

Here are portions of two important letters:

May 31, 1947

Mrs. Franklin D. Roosevelt:

I appreciated very much your letter of the sixteenth and, as you know, my only effort has been to carry out what I thought were the wishes of the late President. . . . There are certain confidential communications which passed between him and some of the heads of states which should not be published at this time. This is particularly true of the correspondence between him and Mr. Stalin. I don't see how he continued as patiently as he did with developments as they were then progressing, but he didn't let his personal feelings enter into his international commitments and the country is certainly lucky that that was the case. . . .

March 16, 1948

MRS. FRANKLIN D. ROOSEVELT:

I think if you will go over the history of the relationship between Russia and us you will find that every effort was made by President Roosevelt and by me to get along with them. Certain agreements were entered into at Tehran and Yalta and so far as our part of those agreements is concerned we carried them out to the letter.

When I arrived at Potsdam for that conference I found that the Poles, at the suggestion of Russia, had moved into eastern Germany and that Russia had taken over a section of eastern Poland. The agreement at Yalta provided for free and untrammeled elections in Rumania, Bulgaria, . . . and Poland. I found a totalitarian Soviet Government set up in Poland, in Rumania, . . . and in Bulgaria. Members of our commissions in Bulgaria and Rumania were treated as if they were stableboys by the Russians in control in those two countries. Russia has not kept faith with us.

I myself discussed the Polish situation with the Polish Government in Potsdam and got no satisfaction whatever from them—yet we made certain agreements in regard to the government of Germany which we have religiously tried to carry out. We have been blocked at every point by the Russians. . . . The Russians have not carried out the agreements entered into at Potsdam. . . . I shall go to the Congress tomorrow and state the facts. Beginning with my Message to the Congress on September 6, 1945, I have constantly informed the Congress and the country of our needs in order to make the United Nations work and to arrive at a peace for the welfare and benefit of every country in the world.

The first decision I had to make after being sworn in at 7:09 P.M., April 12, 1945, was whether to have the United Nations Conference at San Francisco on April 25, 1945. The Charter of the United Nations is a document under which we could work and have peace if we could get Russian cooperation. Twenty-two vetoes have been exercised in the last two and one-half years by the Russian Government. As you know, I had to send Harry Hopkins to see Stalin in order to get Molotov to agree to the fundamental principles of the United Nations Charter.

I am still hopeful and still working with everything I have to make the United Nations work.

Our European Recovery Program and the proper strengthening of our military setup is the only hope we now have for peace in the world. That I am asking from the Congress.

———————

A letter written to Harry H. Woodring, a former Cabinet member in the previous administration, explains itself:

April 30, 1951

HONORABLE HARRY H. WOODRING:

DEAR HARRY: I have just received your good Dale Carnegie letter of April twenty-sixth.

For your information I dictate all my personal letters myself. The one I sent to you was dictated by me and stated the facts just as they are. I am sincerely sorry that you are displeased with the result.

———————

The President often speaks in warm terms of his relationship to three famous Americans who have died in recent years.

Here are some letters he wrote to them:

April 11, 1948

THE HONORABLE CHARLES EVANS HUGHES:

MY DEAR MR. CHIEF JUSTICE: I see you are passing another milestone and I want to congratulate and wish you many happy returns of the day. I hope you will have many more happy birthdays.

You have made a great contribution to the welfare of this great country of ours. I can only wish we had more citizens like you.

March 31, 1951

HON. ARTHUR H. VANDENBERG:

DEAR ARTHUR: I can't tell you how very much I appreciated your good letter of the 29th. You just don't realize what a vacuum there has been in the Senate and in the operation of our foreign policy since you left. That has always been one of the difficulties in the continuation of policy in our government.

I am sincerely hoping that you will recover completely and have an opportunity to train some of the young men in the Senate who are anxious to carry on with what you, Cordell Hull and other Secretaries of State visualized with regard to a continuing foreign policy for this great government of ours.

I mentioned you yesterday in a press conference as one of those who could appreciate exactly what the country needs in its foreign relations.

Personally, I am not confining that need to foreign relations alone. It is very seldom that men really become statesmen while they are yet alive, in the minds of the people and their associates. As you well know, I have always held you in that category.

Take good care of yourself, and if there is anything I can do to contribute to your welfare and recovery, all you need do is name it.

I have had a most pleasant visit down here in Key West, and have succeeded in getting some rest, as much as any President ever gets while he is in office.

Mrs. Truman and Margaret will be here tomorrow to spend next week with me, and then we are going back to Washington to meet the usual grind.

My very best wishes and kindest regards to you and Mrs. Vandenberg.

January 18, 1951

HONORABLE ARTHUR H. VANDENBERG:

DEAR VAN: I certainly did appreciate your good letter of the fifteenth and I am more than happy that you are again out of the hospital.

You will never know how much you are missed down here in Washington. We have had some terrific events take place since your absence from the Senate.

I am hoping that you will soon be fully recovered and that you will take your place as the authority on foreign affairs that you have always assumed in the Senate.

April 9, 1949

HONORABLE HENRY L. STIMSON:

DEAR MR. SECRETARY: I can't tell you how very much I appreciated your cordial note of

April sixth. I am more than happy that you are in agreement with me on the statements made at the signing of the North Atlantic Pact.

We arrived at another milestone day before yesterday in the signing of the agreement with Great Britain and France on a provisional government for the three Western Zones of Germany. I believe these two documents taken together will make a long stride in the direction of peace.

I hope you are in good health and that sometime in the not too far distant future I'll have an opportunity to see you.

My very best to Mrs. Stimson.

July 7, 1950

HONORABLE HENRY L. STIMSON:

DEAR MR. STIMSON: I can't tell you how very much I appreciated your good letter of the fifth.

The situation in Asia has been a very serious one since Japan surrendered. Some agreements were made early in 1943 to keep Russia in the war. Naturally if those agreements had been made after the surrender of Germany and Japan they no doubt would have been arranged in a different manner. I made it my business to try to carry out agreements as they were made when the war was on—maybe that should not have been done but I would still follow that procedure because I believe when agreements are made they should be kept. That is not the policy of the Russian government. From our experience with them they make agreements merely to break them. I think you are correct about Russia being the first one to "wabble on her sticks."

I remember very well your suggestions in the early thirties when Japan went into Manchuria. Had your suggestions been followed I rather think the second world war would not have come about. I was thinking of those things when the decision was made.

I hope everything is going well with you.

———

Here is a letter revealing the President's interest and preoccupation with the establishment of machinery to preserve peace.

November 20, 1950

DEAR MR. ——: Thanks very much for your letter of the tenth, enclosing me a pamphlet on Comparative Laws. Perhaps it never occurred to you that the only time there was a world power, which was centralized in one place, was the time of the Roman Empire and naturally their experience has a great bearing on present day International Law. There is only one material difference, I think, and that is in the approach to criminal procedure. Under the Justinian Code and the Code Napoleon a man is considered guilty unless innocence can be proven. In our approach a man is presumed to be innocent until he is proven guilty. I don't know if that would materially affect International Law as it affects nations.

If we could get the same international application of justice between nations that we have between the states in this Union, I think we could maintain the peace—that is what we are working for at any rate.

I'm interested and appreciate your sending me the pamphlet. I'm no legal scholar, but I've made laws and have enforced them at the local level and now the national and international level. Wish I were the scholar I should be in this position.

––––––––––

Here is a letter, written to the Secretary of the Navy on February 18, 1949, which reveals something of the President's consideration of men:

I have just signed a report from a plucking board which recommended the retirement of a brigadier general in the Marine Corps, and I signed it with reluctance, not because I am personally acquainted with the officer in question but because I don't like this manner of retiring officers, particularly officers with a good war record.

I know that the law provides for this sort of a retirement in Section 314(t) of the Officer Personnel Act of 1947. However, I am not at all pleased with the present legal setup as it affects the retirement of Officers in the Navy and Marine Corps. It seems to me that some sort of procedure could be followed as is followed in the passing over of Officers instead of this forced retirement resorted to by means of a Board.

The brigadier general referred to in this document which I have just signed has an excellent war record. He was considered, in connection with other officers with equally good records in the late war, but the Board has to pick somebody under the law.

I wish you would think about this situation and see if some way can't be found so that officers, who have faithfully served the country for long periods, can't be retired from service without the implication of a blot on their records. It is hard enough on a man to have to retire, after a long period of activity in any line of work, but to be forced into retirement for no good reason except that the finger is pointed at him is likely to give him a complex that will make him unhappy for the rest of his life and I don't think that is fair to a faithful public servant.

Here are two letters which indicate the President's views on economy. The first, beginning sarcastically, is written to a man the President says is a conservative and opposed to the President's views. But the President characterized the recipients of this letter and the letter that follows as men whose points of view he always solicits to check against his own views and information.

April 20, 1949

I am certainly sorry that we are frightening all the good old ladies who control the money in the country, if what you say is true.

I fear very much that you still have your economic royalist viewpoint and are not particularly interested in the welfare of the vast majority of people. It is my business to see that everybody gets a fair deal and that is exactly what I am trying to do.

I am more than glad to hear from you and to have your viewpoint on things.

February 28, 1949

I appreciated very much your letter of the twenty-first and I am happy to get your viewpoint on the situation.

It seems rather peculiar to me that the effort of the Government to act as referee in the interest of business is always considered too much interference. A lack of proper interference in the 1920s brought about the most terrible of all depressions. Due to the policy pursued in the last fourteen years the Democratic Administration has been responsible for the restoration of the most stable period in our economy, regardless of the fact that the war had a great deal to do with the high price era through which we have been going.

I sincerely hope that I can count on you and your advice and cooperation to help stabilize the situation so that we can have full employment and good profits. Both have been very much in evidence the last two years, and if business doesn't go haywire and become afraid and confused I think we are faced with a continuance of that same prospect.

I am more than happy to have your views frankly stated on the subject—that is exactly what I want.

Here follow four typical letters to legislators:

January 2, 1951

HONORABLE HARRY F. BYRD
UNITED STATES SENATOR

DEAR HARRY: I appreciated most highly your letter of the twenty-second. I've always tried my best to make the revenue meet the expenses of the Government and had it not been for the action of the 80th Congress there never would have been a deficit in any year for which I have sent a Budget to the Congress. Present conditions are such now, however, that it is necessary to tax until it hurts. Expenditures for the general Government have never been excessive or extravagant. It has been my privilege to help with the making of ten Budgets while I was in the Senate and I've made five since I've been President. I am now working on another and there is never a figure goes into the Budget message that I am not familiar with.

I am very highly pleased with your pledge of support in the present emergency. I don't think there has ever been any serious difference between us on the operations of the Government except maybe in some policy approaches on which we naturally would not agree.

Thanks very much for your kind letter.

August 13, 1951

HONORABLE CLARENCE CANNON
UNITED STATES REPRESENTATIVE

DEAR CLARENCE: The Clerk of the Armed Services Subcommittee of the House Committee on Appropriations has requested certain information with regard to the aircraft used by the President. There has been a great deal of talk about this aircraft and about the Presidential yacht. Most of it, as you know, is political "hooey" but if you, yourself, are interested in the actual expense of the aircraft assigned for Presidential use, and the amount of use which the President makes of it, I will be glad to give it to you.

This aircraft is used principally for bringing and returning heads of states to the United States. The Presidents of Brazil, Chile, Ecuador, Mexico, France and the Shah of Iran have all been transported in this plane. It has other uses besides that and it is necessary that the crew have certain flying hours. It is impossible for me as President to keep certain engagements, such as the one in Detroit and the one which I will have to keep in San Francisco on the fourth day of September, unless a rapid means of transportation is at the President's beck and call.

It seems that this is rather a petty approach to embarrass the President. It is on the same level with Senator Williams' cut of the Presidential appropriation for the operation of the White House. When that was done, of course, the Congress increased the legislative appropriation by enough to meet all of the raises and increases that were necessary.

I will be glad to talk with you and the Chairman of the Subcommittee, who is interested in this matter, if you want to come up here with him.

March 22, 1948

Honorable Lyndon B. Johnson
United States Representative

Dear Lyndon: Thanks a lot for your letter of the twentieth. The matter to which you refer has been taken care of by the contracts under which these properties are sold to private individuals. In a case of emergency they immediately revert to the Government.

If the Congress would act on the measures which I have asked for there would be no necessity for any world emergency. As you know, these measures were asked for in November 1945—again the problem was gone over in the State of the Union Message of 1946; also in the spring of 1946. They were reiterated in the fall of 1946 and again in the State of the Union Message of 1947, but apparently this country never looks ahead in its international relations until the actual emergency comes forward. If there was a little less emergency talk and a little more activity on the part of the Congress to meet the international problem we would be able to meet it.

I hope you will put your shoulder to the wheel and help get those measures I asked for on the statute books—that is the only way to meet this situation.

February 18, 1949

Honorable Edwin C. Johnson
United States Senator

Dear Ed: I read your letter of the fourteenth with some surprise. It is not the habit of people in my immediate office to make any suggestions to quasi-judicial boards. You know the Congress creates the boards—the President appoints them and they have specific duties by law. They are supposed to be made up of men of integrity who weigh facts and they should not be importuned individually to do special favors.

My only appearances before these boards while I was in the Senate were public appearances, usually at the request of the boards to express my opinion. I remember three specific instances in which I appeared before boards of this sort.

I once appeared before the Interstate Commerce Commission and made a statement of my views on the sale of railroad securities. It is a matter of record. I didn't discuss my views with any single member of the Interstate Commerce Commission but stated them in public before the whole commission.

I made a similar appearance before the Securities and Exchange Commission to discuss the same question, and I appeared before the Communications Commission to discuss what I thought was the proper way of handling applications for radio stations. All these were public appearances and are of record.

Never in my ten years in the Senate did I ever lobby with any commission for a special interest in my own state or any other state. I think it is bad policy for Senators and Representatives or representatives of the President to lobby with these commissions and boards. I have no intention of bringing pressure to bear on any one of these commissions for any purpose whatever. If the people on the boards and commissions, appointed by the President and confirmed by the Senate, are not men enough and ethical enough to transact the business of the Government they ought not to be on the Boards. It is their business to find the facts and make decisions.

I have had to reorganize the Civil Aeronautics Board because of so many special interests lobbying with them and those special interests work from every angle.

I have been told that there are more lobbyists in Washington than any other city and that they receive five or six times the pay that the five hundred and thirty-one members of the Congress receive. I think that is rather disgraceful and, in my opinion, that is something the Congress really ought to do something about.

VI

"Where there is corruption, there are always the corrupters," said the President, as he began to express his views on ethics and morals in public affairs.

"There would be no corruption if it were not for the corrupters. There are always weak people in every human setup. The human animal is built that way. When the golden apple is dangled before them, some take a bite out of it, and some eat the whole apple.

"We must find a way to make the corrupter as guilty legally as the one who is corrupted. This would go a long way in solving a serious problem in public life. We need to expose and convict the rascals who today conduct their dirty business with virtual immunity. We need stringent legislation to deal with the menace of the tempter as well as the tempted.

"I have always felt deeply about this subject of corruption. There is nothing I detest so much as a crooked politician or corrupt government official. But the type of businessman who is a fixer is even lower in my estimation.

"These are the termites that undermine respect for government and confidence in government and cast doubt on the vast majority of honest and hardworking federal officials.

"Some dishonest people worm themselves into almost every organization. It is all the more shocking when they make their way into our kind of government which is based on the principle of justice to all. That is why I shall see to it that any federal employee, guilty of misconduct, is removed and punished.

"But I intend to protect with equal vigor the vast majority of federal employees who are honest, loyal and hardworking public servants, against irresponsible and misinformed critics.

"There are those who suggest that all federal employees must bear the burden of always seeming right in addition to being right. I go along with this exacting standard. But I will not allow any man to be punished for not seeming to be right if in fact he is not wrong.

"Long before the headlines screamed about corruption, the government had been taking steps to remove wrongdoers, wherever there was evidence. This is a never ending job of the government.

"We need the help of everyone to prevent improper conduct in the public service and to protect the government from the insidious influence peddlers and favor seekers.

"We must meet all possible avenues of corruption. I think that every public official that gets more than ten thousand dollars a year ought to show exactly what his outside income is, if he has any. That should include district attorneys, Senators and Congressmen and everyone in the federal service.

"I don't see any reason why that shouldn't be done. If a fellow is honest, he doesn't care. Some people have asked whether this would not be considered an invasion of the private rights of government officials. I don't think so. There is no reason why they shouldn't show where their income is coming from.

"One of the most important steps to be taken in dealing with the whole problem of corruption in public life is to put key government officials under civil service.

"I recommended that collectors of internal revenue be replaced by officials operating under civil service.

"And I have directed that a study be made to see if we cannot make district attorneys and United States marshals subject to civil service. Deputy U. S. marshals are now civil service men, but marshals are not.

"There is going to be a howl from the patronage boys all the way down the street. But I will fight for this vital and urgent change."

BLAIR HOUSE

WITH SECRETARY OF STATE DEAN ACHESON

VII

"A direct statement of the facts without trimmings and without oratory."

This is President Truman's idea of what a speech should be.

"People want to know the facts," he said. "Most everybody now has the fundamentals of an education, even if all are not highly educated, and people understand things without the trimmings. People don't go to hear people make speeches for entertainment any more. They have plenty of entertainment on the radio, and television and the movies. What they want are facts and supporting data to prove those facts are correct, and that's all there is to it."

The making of speeches is, of course, one of the other great problems of the Presidency. No President has ever benefited more or suffered more from speechmaking than Mr. Truman.

When the President speaks without notes he is effective and easy in manner.

"Often when I have to read a speech I feel strained," he explained. "Sometimes people think that when I feel this strain I am not acquainted with the speech I am making. That isn't so. I take great pains with every formal speech I make and frequently as many as seven and eight drafts are gone over by me before the final version is completed. I'm just not a polished speaker and reading a text sometimes handicaps natural emphasis.

"But I follow the practice of many speakers and radio commentators by underlining certain sentences or phrases or even words which I wish to emphasize.

"But all too frequently I can't resist making a penciled mark on the margin of the text I am going to read from for an off the cuff remark.

"Sometimes I forget the microphone and the formality and really warm up. But you will note it's usually where I want to drive home some important facts and not just phraseology. Ever since I've been President I have had more offers of help from speech writers and coiners of phrases, all of whom guaranteed that I could really become a great orator. But I don't believe in words for word's sake.

"Where I have no text in front of me and I'm free to talk as I would to you across the table then I do better. The campaign of 1948 showed that. The people wanted to hear what I had to say, and whether I meant what I said.

"It takes special talent to be a speaker.

"But everybody can tell whether a man is sincere or knows what he's talking about without his having to have that special talent and that's what counts.

"But speechmaking is an important part of my duties, especially on statements to the people on urgent domestic and foreign policy matters."

I asked the President to explain the routine of how the making of speeches is decided on and how they are written.

He said:

"Naturally there are many invitations for the President to speak. He has to be careful that he selects a forum that is dignified and feels that a speech before this forum will be of value in throwing light on what he or the government is doing.

"The subject is chosen depending upon the circumstance of time and background.

"I then suggest an outline to my staff and the staff goes and does the essential research and gets the detailed information. A rough draft is drawn up and then we discuss it around the table. Probably as many as a half dozen drafts follow, each one of which is not only discussed jointly but which I mark up. I then decide upon a final draft and the speech is typed and ready for delivery.

"Sometimes I have taken a final draft to my study and during the night have rewritten many pages. And very frequently just an hour or two before delivery I have made last-minute alterations on what we call the master copy because I have thought of some simpler words to use.

"Take for instance the San Francisco speech after my visit to Wake Island to see General MacArthur. The speech was discussed very thoroughly in Honolulu and was worked over on the plane. Then I spent the whole day and half the night going over it and making changes in the final form. I imagine it had been gone over twenty times.

"This San Francisco speech was an important policy speech and needed to be checked for example by the State Department among others. The speech I made in San Francisco on a later trip on politics to a group of Western Democratic leaders I wrote out entirely by hand with pen. This I did with comparative ease since all the points I wanted to make were strong in my mind. Another instance of a policy speech is the one I made regarding Russia and world peace at Winston-Salem, North Carolina, on October 15, 1951, in connection with the ground-breaking ceremonies for Wake Forest College. My speech was followed up by an important statement of our policy on disarmament by Dean Acheson before the United Nations."

military orders actually under production in your factories. A year

from now we'll really be seeing great quantities of equipment rolling

off your assembly lines. By then we will have more steel and more

of almost every other material for both military and civilian

production.

When we have done that, we will have passed another great

milestone on our way to peace in the world. We will still have a long

way to go, and there will [still] be dangers ahead, but we should be a

[good deal] closer to the time when the clouds of fear that now over-

shadow the world will be swept away.

This past year has been a period that has challenged and

tested all we have done since the end of World War II to bring about

peace in the world. The aggression in Korea was aimed at the whole

idea of the United Nations. It was intended to pick off one free

nation after another. It was intended to create fear

and scare the rest into submission. We could have given up

in the face of that attack. We could have abandoned the United

Nations, torn up the Charter, and retreated into a hopeless and fear-

ful isolation. But we didn't do that.

We went forward. We picked up the challenge and hurled it

back. The United Nations did not go under. It hung together, and

today it is stronger than it has ever been. Today, the Charter seems

---

President's Speech Opening
San Francisco Conference

I am glad to welcome you to this conference for the signing

of the Treaty of Peace with Japan. The people of the United States

are honored to serve as hosts for this meeting.

Six years have now passed since the last shot was fired in

the war against Japanese aggression. We are meeting here to bring

that war to a formal conclusion.

It is our purpose to lay the foundation for lasting peace

in the future. We do not wish to dwell upon the grievances of the

past. We fought a bitter and costly war against Japan to defend our

countries and to preserve our freedom. But we did not fight in a

spirit of vengeance or conquest.

The principles for which we fought were clearly set forth

by President Franklin D. Roosevelt when the United States declared

war upon Japan. On December 9, 1941, in a broadcast to the American

people, President Roosevelt said:

"When we resort to force, as now we must, we are determined

that this force shall be directed toward ultimate good as well

as against immediate evil.... We are now in the midst of a war,

---

July 26, 1951

Memorandum for The President

Here is a draft of the Detroit

speech. We will be working on it in

the Cabinet Room tonight if you want

to get in touch with us.

C. S. Murphy

Charlie - I am returning
this with some markings
I have not gone over the
other section, but I will
soon as I've had my
dinner. Looks as if we
will come up with a good one
HT

---

but Dean Acheson's job has been to bring whole nations over to our

side, to fight with us if there is a showdown -- and that's exactly

what he's done! And it's a lot more than his detractors have ever

done for their country. Dean's detractors are the worst
slackers this nation ever produced!

That kind of political smear is doing this country No good.

good. It's playing right into the hands of the Russians. It's time

it was stopped. Lies, slander, mud are the weapons
of the totalitarians. No man of morals or ethics
will use them. As far as I am concerned, there ought to be no Democrats

and no Republicans in the field of foreign policy. We are all Americans,
citizens of the greatest republic in history.
We have had a bi-partisan foreign policy in this country since Pearl

Harbor. I would like to keep it. I know lots of Republicans anniversary!

who want to keep it that way -- Republicans working in the Administration,

and in the Congress, and outside in the country.

I say to them -- this is the time, now, to show your true

colors -- to show the real loyalty of the Republican party to the

great ideals on which this country is founded. Now is the time to

put a stop to the sordid efforts some Republicans are making to find

political gain by stirring up fear and distrust about our foreign

policy. Now is the time to say to the dividers and confusers -- no

renegade Democrats

Here are some extracts from a few formal speeches the President has made which illustrate the style of his approach to various types of audiences. The themes vary from his spiritual beliefs to his political beliefs.

ADDRESS OF THE PRESIDENT

To the Washington Pilgrimage of American Churchmen
At the National City Christian Church, Washington, D. C.

September 28, 1951

Mr. Chairman, Dr. Pruden, my friends:

I am happy to have the privilege of speaking to this meeting of the Washington Pilgrimage of American Churchmen. You have come to the nation's capital to visit its monuments and to look at the basic documents on which our government was founded. Many people come to Washington to do these things, but you have come here for a special purpose. You have come here to emphasize the fact that this nation was founded on religious principles.

You will see, as you make your rounds, that this nation was established by men who believed in God. You will see that our founding fathers believed that God created this nation. And I believe it, too. They believed that God was our strength in time of peril and the source of our blessings.

You will see the evidence of this deep religious faith on every hand.

If we go back to the Declaration of Independence, we notice that it was drawn up by men who believed that God the Creator had made all men equal and had given them certain rights which no man could take away from them. In beginning their great enterprise, the signers of the Declaration of Independence entrusted themselves to the protection of Divine Providence.

To our forefathers, it seemed something of a miracle that this nation was able to go through the agonies of the American Revolution and emerge triumphant. They saw, in our successful struggle for independence, the working of God's hand. In his first inaugural address, George Washington said, "No people can be bound to acknowledge and adore the invisible hand, which conducts the affairs of men, more than the people of the United States."

Another fact which you will notice in the course of your pilgrimage is that the makers of our Constitution believed in religious toleration. Theirs was the highest type of religion, forbidding the use of coercion or force in matters of mind and spirit. Religious freedom was a part of their religious faith. And they received that from Roger Williams the Baptist, from William Penn, a Quaker; and from Lord Baltimore, a Catholic. That's the reason for our constitutional approach to religious freedom.

It is said that when Benjamin Franklin left the Constitutional Convention he was asked, "What have you given us?" He answered, "A republic, if you can keep it." Millions of Americans since then have believed that the keeping of our Republic depends upon keeping the deep religious convictions on which it was founded. From the worship and teachings of the synagogues and churches of our land, have come a moral integrity, a concern for justice and human welfare, a sense of human equality, and a love of human freedom, and a practice of brotherhood which are necessary to the life of our national institutions.

ADDRESS OF THE PRESIDENT

Before the National Association of Postmasters in Constitution Hall

September 17, 1951.

I am very glad to welcome you to Washington.

I don't believe there is a finer group of public servants anywhere than the members of the postal service.

There are some people, I suppose, who would call this just a meeting of bureaucrats. Well, if you are bureaucrats, I am a bureaucrat too, and proud of it.

It seems to be open season, these days, on government employees. There are a lot of people who are trying to make political capital by slurring the loyalty and efficiency of government employees, and trying to bring the public service into disrepute.

I think that is a contemptible way to try to get votes.

We have the greatest government in the world, and the most loyal and efficient government servants. I am proud to be a part of it. I think you are proud to be part of it, too.

It is time we made it perfectly plain that we feel it is an honor to work for our fellow citizens through the public service.

The postal service is one of the key activities of the Federal Government. It employs over half a million people, one fourth of all the civilian employees of the whole government. It is one of the biggest businesses in the country. And without it, the rest of the country would not be able to do business at all. Without the postal service all our activities would come to a standstill—business, the national defense, family life, everything.

LOOKING FROM LINCOLN MEMORIAL TOWARD THE WASHINGTON
MONUMENT AND THE CAPITOL

ADDRESS OF THE PRESIDENT

To the Attorney Generals' Conference On Law Enforcement Problems
Department of Justice Auditorium, Washington, D. C.

February 15, 1950.

Mr. Attorney General, and gentlemen of the Conference:

When the Attorney General told me of his plan to hold this Conference, I welcomed the idea. It seemed to me that it would be most useful for federal, state and local officials concerned with law enforcement problems to gather together to devise ways and means of making law enforcement better and more effective.

There has been a substantial postwar increase in crime in this country, particularly in crimes of violence. This is disturbing, but it is one of the inevitable results of war, and the dislocations that spring from war. It is one of the many reasons why we must work with other nations for a permanent peace.

I might remind you that after every war this country has ever been engaged in, we have had exactly the same problems to face. After the Revolutionary War, we had almost exactly the same problems with which we are faced now, out of which came the Alien and Sedition Acts, which we finally had to repeal because they did not agree with the Bill of Rights. Then, after the War between the States, or the Civil War, we had all sorts of banditry. My state was famous for some of the great bandits of that time, if you recall. We had the same situation after World War One. We had a terrible time then, with the increase in crimes of violence. We managed to handle the situation, and I am just as sure as I stand here that we will do it again.

This postwar increase in crime has been accompanied by a resurgence of underworld forces—forces which thrive on vice and greed. This underworld has used its resources to corrupt the moral fiber of some of our citizens and some of our communities. It carries a large share of the responsibility for the general increase in crime in the last few years.

This is a problem that, in one degree or another, affects every community in the country, and every level of government. Our rural areas as well as our cities are involved in this.

It is important, therefore, that we work together in combating organized crime in all its forms. We must use our courts and our law enforcement agencies, and the moral forces of our people, to put down organized crime wherever it appears.

At the same time, we must aid and encourage gentler forces to do their work of prevention and cure. These forces include education, religion, and home training, family and child guidance, and wholesome recreation.

The most important business in this nation—or any other nation, for that matter—is raising and training children. If those children have the proper environment at home, and educationally, very, very few of them ever turn out wrong. I don't think we put enough stress on the necessity of implanting in the child's mind the moral code under which we live.

The fundamental basis of this nation's law was given to Moses on the Mount. The fundamental basis of our Bill of Rights comes from the teachings which we get from Exodus and St. Matthew, from Isaiah and St. Paul. I don't think we emphasize that enough these days.

If we don't have the proper fundamental moral background, we will finally wind up with a totalitarian government which does not believe in rights for anybody except the state.

Above all, we must recognize that human misery breeds most of our crime. We must wipe out our slums, improve the health of our citizens, and eliminate the inequalities of opportunity which embitter men and women and turn them toward lawlessness. In the long run, these programs represent the greatest of all anti-crime measures.

And I want to emphasize particularly equality of opportunity. I think every child in the nation, regardless of his race, creed or color, should have the right to a proper education. And when he has finished that education, he ought to have the right in industry to fair treatment in employment. If he is able and willing to do the job, he ought to be given a chance to do that job, no matter what his religious connections are, or what his color is.

REMARKS OF THE PRESIDENT

At a Luncheon of Democrats from Eleven Western States
Gold Room, Fairmont Hotel, San Francisco, California

September 4, 1951.

Madam Chairman, fellow Democrats, distinguished guests:

I am most happy to be here today. I was here sometime ago when the United Nations was organized, and opened its first regular meeting. It was a great privilege. That organization, I am sure, will eventually cause us to have world peace.

I came here for the purpose of opening the Conference for the signing of the treaty of peace with Japan. I can only be here for the day, but I couldn't possibly turn down the opportunity to talk to some of my Democratic brethren and sisters.

Fairmont Hotel
NOB HILL
San Francisco

I intend to keep right on fighting for ~~to bring~~ the means to join with our allies in proper arrangements for our common defense against all aggressors.

I intend to keep right on fighting to build an economically strong country at home — one in which the people will get the benefit.

I don't believe in government for special privilege! Our resources should be used for the benefit of all the people.

When we produce electric power at Shasta Dam, when we ~~keep~~ develop the Roanoke Basin in Virginia, it ought to be for the benefit of the people — not for the benefit of private power companies.

The Democratic Party stands for the people, and for the public interest — and we'll keep the Party that way.

The opposition has plenty of money and powerful connections in Washington, ready

You know, it is good to get together with a group of Democrats, especially an enthusiastic group like this.

I had some experience here in this town in 1948—had a wonderful meeting down in front of City Hall in San Francisco. And the result was very satisfactory.

You in this city witnessed the first great step toward lasting peace back in 1945 when the United Nations Charter was signed here. During the six years since then, we have been working constantly for world peace. Step by step we will keep on working for peace. We are building up our armed strength here at home just to keep the peace, and we are helping our friends to build up their strength, for the simple purpose to keep the peace.

We are trying to accomplish the purposes for which the United Nations was established—negotiation of differences between nations, instead of shooting at each other to settle their differences.

It is terrible to think of what would happen if we should have another world war. No one can imagine the destruction, the loss of life.

New weapons mean that an all-out war would wipe out civilization. It is the job of every American—be he Democrat or Republican—to do all he can to prevent all-out war.

There are a lot of people who do not seem to understand this. There are a lot of people who will not or cannot understand the world situation and the problems we face. There are a lot of people who are not willing to pay the taxes and appropriate the necessary money it takes to arm ourselves and our allies.

And you know, we must have friends and allies, and we must help to arm them to keep the peace in the world.

I say to you that these people are flirting with national suicide—flirting with the end of civilization and the return to the darkest of the dark ages.

It is fantastic what can happen with the use of new weapons that are now under construction in this country, not only the one which we all fear the most, but there are some weapons which are fantastic in their operation.

I hope we will never have to use them.

The President handed me the full text of the above political speech as he had written it in his own handwriting. He said: "I wrote this on hotel stationery."

I commented on the simple sentences and then told him that a publisher friend of mine had remarked: "Truman's style sometimes reminds me of the style of Cicero."

The President looked at me with an owlish look in his eyes and then laughed, saying: "I have tried to imitate Cicero but I can't. I have read all of Cicero's orations in Latin. Charlie Ross and I used to translate them together. I think the two outstanding orators in the history of the world were Demosthenes and Cicero."

Later I found among the President's private papers these two excerpts copied out in his own hand.

These are comments on the retirement of Lucullus. Lucullus lived from 110 B.C. to 57 or 56 B.C.)

—the administration of public affairs has, like other things its proper term, and statesmen as well as wrestlers will break down, when strength and youth fail.

Better . . . had it been for Cicero, after Catiline's conspiracy, to have retired and grown old, and for Scipio, after his Numantine and Carthaginian conquests, to have sat down contented.

Life of Lucullus, Plutarch
Translated by Giles Thornburgh, A.M.

It is necessary for him who would dexterously govern a commonwealth, in action, always to prefer that which is honest before that which is popular, and in speaking, to free the right and useful measure from everything that may occasion offense.

Cicero was one man, above all others, who made the Romans feel how great a charm eloquence lends to what is good, and how invincible justice is, if it be well spoken.

Plutarch's Lives — Life of Cicero
Translated by Thomas Fuller

Every time the President spoke to me of speeches he kept stressing the need for simplicity of style.

He said: "We have had some excellent writers of simple English in this country. Mark Twain's *Tom Sawyer* is an outstanding example of the simplest way to say things so that people can understand them. If I were going to cultivate a style of writing, I would try to make it as simple as possible and straightforward, and state the facts as they are. That was Cicero's way. He stated his case, and then he argued it and that is all there was to it.

"I never had any reputation as a speaker at all until the 1948 campaign. Of course, I had spoken all over the state of Missouri to convince people I was right on four different occasions. But as for style in speaking or writing, I never had any. Whatever style I had just came naturally, just a natural outgrowth. But I love the style of the Bible, the King James' version of the Bible. It is the finest and most stately brand of English there is."

STARTING FOR AN EARLY MORNING WALK

VIII

One evening the President said:

"You have been asking a lot of questions. Now let me put a hypothetical question to you. Suppose that Franklin Roosevelt had died between the November election and the Inauguration on January 20, 1945. What would have happened?"

I replied: "You would have become President."

Mr. Truman said: "No, that isn't so. I had not been sworn in as Vice President. Vice President Henry Wallace would have succeeded to the Presidency. With Mr. Wallace as President, there would have been no Vice President, because I couldn't have been sworn in until January 20. And then I would have become only the Vice President. That is a flaw in our Constitutional Law. There would have been considerable legal and political debate but the fact is that we would not have had a clear-cut definite procedure by which a President could have been chosen at such a time.

"When I succeeded President Roosevelt, one of my first concerns was to get through Congress a law dealing with the succession of Presidents. I felt then that where there is no Vice President the man who succeeds to the Presidency should be as nearly as possible an elected official instead of the Secretary of State, an appointee of the President, as previously provided. The Speaker of the House, who is the most powerful man in the government aside from the President, is more nearly elected by the whole country than any other man. As a representative he is an elected official of his constituency. To be chosen as Speaker of the House, he is elected by the majority of the House of Representatives.

"Such a law was passed.

"But I have been thinking recently that we ought to have an even clearer method. Perhaps this may be the solution: that when the President dies and the Vice President succeeds, why not call the electors who have elected the President and Vice President by the mandate of the people at the polls, and have them elect a new Vice President."

WITH VICE PRESIDENT ALBEN W. BARKLEY

IX

I asked President Truman if he would summarize for me what he considered the most important achievements of his administration. The year 1951 was drawing to a close and Mr. Truman had been in the White House six years and eight months.

The President replied:

"We have prevented a third world war. And we have kept American economy on an even keel. The Russians had the idea that after 1946 we would explode and then the Russians could have had the world to themselves. We have managed to keep that from happening."

PART TWO

Student of History

I

"There is nothing new in the world except the history you do not know."

President Truman went on to explain what he meant.

"No, there is not really anything new, if you know what has gone before. What is new to people is what they do not know about their history or the history of the world.

"The human animal hasn't changed much since the beginning. For example, there was greed even between Cain and Abel. The laws of the ancients had to meet the same sort of situations and problems that we face now. I do not think that there is as great a percentage of fundamentally crooked people now as there was in the Middle Ages. I think the most scandalous period ever in the history of the world was the Dark Ages, because the people did not have the education and the background to know what was right from wrong.

"I'm a great optimist about people and their future. But it's not enough to know history without doing something about the future.

"This Republic of ours is probably the accumulation of all the experiences of the Roman republic and the Greek idea of free speech and the British contribution in the form of the bill of rights. Another country will eventually come along that may be greater than ours but meanwhile we have got to make our contribution. And we are making our contribution in helping to fight for peace and bring about the proper development of all the resources of the world, so that people everywhere can have something more important to do than murdering each other. At least that is what I hope for—what we hope for—and hope is no good without some work. You've got to work for it."

I said: "You often draw parallels from history, Mr. President. Can you give me one or two?"

"Well," he said, "take Darius the Great of Persia. Darius was one of the greatest ad-

[81]

ministrators in the history of the world, a statesman and an organizer. He used a method that will work any time. He let the people over whom he ruled have as much say as possible, and yet kept his hands on things.

"And then he made one fundamental mistake. He got to thinking that the Scythians on the Volga River were a menace to him, and he thought he would put them out of business. Darius would have been a success if he had not gone into Russia and the Russian Steppes. But he couldn't make it any more than centuries later Napoleon or Hitler could. The reason is simple.

"When you try to conquer other people or extend yourself over vast areas you cannot win in the long run.

"Take some recent history.

"Hitler wanted to' control the whole of Europe, just as Napoleon did. If Napoleon hadn't gone into Russia, he would have remained master of Europe. When Hitler went into Russia, he showed he didn't know his history well enough. He had made a deal with Soviet Russia that might have stood up. But he lost everything by invasion. If he hadn't invaded, he might have won something, perhaps, because the Ukrainians and the White Russians wanted to join Hitler, but he treated them like dogs and slaves. He looked on them as an inferior people. And he paid for that.

"The Russians today foolishly think that we are imperialistic and want to conquer their land. The very opposite is true. They are the imperialists. We are not imperialists. We do not want any more territory. We do not want to conquer any people. We want to help people because helping them means helping ourselves.

"We know the Russians are a menace to us and that is why we are building up our strength, not to march against them, but to discourage them from marching against us and the free world.

"Let's go back into ancient history again.

"Alexander the Great made the same mistake of expanding and conquering. He stretched himself all the way to India. And then the people around him made him think he was immortal, and he found that thirty-three quarts of wine was too much for any man, and it killed him at Babylon. It was too bad, because he had a lot of good qualities.

"The same thing happened to the Roman emperors. There was one of them I admire immensely, Marcus Aurelius Antoninus. He not only was a great field general, but he was a thinker and a philosopher, a Stoic philosopher. Some of his precepts and thoughts on ethical and moral standards are similar to our own idea of what is right and what is wrong. In his 'Meditations' he said a man must cultivate four virtues: wisdom, justice, fortitude and moderation. He must have been a very great man.

"There were six or eight great Roman emperors; and as many who weren't.

ALEXANDER THE GREAT   JULIUS CAESAR

"Imperialists never win in the long run. Take Caesar and Napoleon. They were failures because they wanted to expand their domain.

"Contrast that with our objective, with the American aim. We want to help people to help themselves, because that makes for prosperity for everyone. And we can learn a lot from other people. There are many things that even the so-called backward people in the world can teach us. We must exchange ideas. We must exchange goods.

"The history of the world has been founded on world trade. When people exchanged their handicraft and goods and food, populations grew and spread, and civilization developed.

"I believe if we could help people today to develop the undeveloped places of the world, we would not have to worry about our own great industrial machine, which would have so much to do, and it would also help other people. We must never forget that prosperity for other people means prosperity for us and prosperity for us means prosperity for other people.

"There are three forces at work in the world today. There is Russian imperialism—and it isn't much different from the Czarist imperialism.

"Then there is the international Communist conspiracy, which Russian imperialism uses to inflame resurgent fanatical nationalisms.

"And then there is the combined force of hunger, want and insecurity that puts fear in the hearts of people and makes them feel that something is going to go wrong in the world.

"Those three forces, working together, make it very difficult for us to achieve what we are trying to do; which is nothing in the world but gaining happiness for everybody."

I interrupted the President to ask him:

"Do you think we can overcome this great fear the people have?"

The President got up from his desk and went over to the globe again.

He said: "Yes, I do. Yes, I do. I think there is a very good possibility of overcoming it. That is the end I am working toward all the time. That is the end we are all working for. Maybe we cannot achieve our aim fully in this generation or even in the next, but we can set the wheels rolling which will bring us there and that is the important thing.

"You know, in 1847 or 1848 or thereabouts, when Lord Russell was Prime Minister of England, the Duke of Wellington, who earlier had been Prime Minister, is supposed to have said that he was glad he was going to die because the British Empire was on the way out.

"Yet the greatest period of the British Empire was yet to come after he had died—with Gladstone and Disraeli building a greater British Empire.

"There are some people who say that this great Republic of ours is on the way out. They don't know what they are talking about. We are only at the beginning of very great things and I do not mean in the imperialistic sense. I can't say this too often: imperialism never is successful and certainly won't work in the modern world."

I asked, "Do you think war can be prevented by men? What role do you think men play in history in relation to events?"

The President had come back to his desk. He is an active man, but not a restless one. Frequently when he sits expounding ideas his body is relaxed and quiet, even his hands are at rest. His face, however, mirrors many moods and is forever changing. My question, I could see, bringing tension in the line of his lips, was one that stirred him, for this was a subject to which he frequently returned in the many talks I had with him.

He said: "Well, all the great—those we call great—like Alexander and Caesar and Napoleon, and those pretenders to greatness, like Hitler and Mussolini and Lenin—based their powers on war and the results of war.

"The Russian revolution came about through weakness and corruption of the Czarist regime. Hitler's rise to power was due to the feeling of the German people that they had been terribly mistreated in the first world war and they wanted to get back on top. Mussolini took over a situation in Italy verging on anarchy. But Mussolini himself ended in anarchy and Hitler came to the same bad end.

"I am hoping that sometime or other the Sermon on the Mount will sink in and that we can get something done. I hope we can make Stalin realize that we believe in that Sermon on the Mount and that as a realist, he ought to do as he would be done by."

I pointed to the many books on history in his library and among them recent publications.

The President said:

"Sometimes I get a chance to read them. My favorite pastime is to check on dates and men.

"I wonder how many know what a great man King Henry the Fourth of France, King Henry of Navarre was? I, myself, think he was the greatest of the French kings. The Grand Plan of Henry the Fourth must have given Woodrow Wilson the idea for a League of Nations, because the Grand Plan, or 'Great Design,' proposed an international union of rulers to keep the peace.

"Some historians say that King Henry the Fourth didn't work out so noble a plan, but I think he did. He was assassinated about the time he got ready to carry out his program, just as Lincoln was assassinated at the time he was most needed.

"I can't understand why men like these are opposed for their good deeds and assassinated. If only people would get away from fighting each other. If only they would be interested in developing their own countries instead of quarreling among themselves. Things would be so much better with the proper development of the resources of a country than in always planning to murder each other. The simple truth is hard to learn and that is, it is in the interest of people to keep the peace.

"Someday we may get to that. We must."

I said, "That is what we hope for."

Mr. Truman replied, "Well, hope is no good without work. We have got to work for it."

I asked him whether in his reading of history he found a tendency of mankind or civilization to improve.

The President said, "There is no doubt about it.

"History is a story of improvement even if there are setbacks. There was an improvement from the time of Hammurabi and Rameses to Rome, and when Rome blew up, then everything went back a thousand years.

"Since the Renaissance there has been a constant improvement.

"But another world war would put civilization back some thousand years or more."

II

President Truman said:

"If a man is acquainted with what other people have experienced at this desk it will be easier for him to go through a similar experience. It is ignorance that causes most mistakes. The man who sits here ought to know his American history, at least."

President Truman probably knows as much about the history of the Presidency as any man who ever sat in the White House. He has been a close student of the conduct and ideas of every President, even to the extent of knowing what practically every cabinet officer since Washington's time did to help or hinder the functioning of the Presidency. There is hardly a problem confronting him today for which he cannot quickly cite a parallel in the past.

The President continued:

"But, as I have been pointing out to you, it is not enough to know just American history. The trouble with some specialists in history is that they write about one country or one period as if nothing else existed in the world. Imagine writing a history of the United States without reference to Europe or Asia. Who today can write or think about the United States or the American continents as isolated from the rest of the world. An American President today must take into account things that happen far beyond our own frontiers."

I asked the President, "What Presidents have had the greatest influence on you?"

He replied, "Well, the two most important ones are Jefferson and Jackson. Jefferson

THOMAS JEFFERSON   ANDREW JACKSON

made the people the government, and Jackson re-established the government of the people.

"Washington, Jefferson, Jackson, Lincoln, Hayes, Cleveland, Woodrow Wilson and Franklin Delano Roosevelt were strong presidents. Washington made the federal government strong. Lincoln saved the Union and the Republic as one nation indivisible. Hayes restored the Lincoln plan of forgiving the secessionist.

"Cleveland represents the idea that one party cannot forever control a great republic.

"Wilson, a great historian, understood that global affairs affected the United States. The fact that he couldn't put over his great idea at the time killed him.

"Franklin Roosevelt took the Wilson idea, and, in the Atlantic Charter and the United Nations organization, started the world on a road to peace.

"The first President, George Washington, was one of the best administrators that ever sat at this desk. He was a real organizer. Cleveland was a great administrator, but only during his first term. He failed in his second administration. The difficulty with him was that he wanted to do everything himself. He was, because of that, one of the hardest working presidents.

"A man who did as much as any President for his country, but one you do not hear much about, is Rutherford B. Hayes. Hayes, in my opinion, was elected by fraud. The Congress did not follow out its constitutional obligations in the election of Hayes. Congress appointed a commission to review the voting in four states and the commission, making its decision strictly on a political basis, and not on the facts, chose Hayes. If Tilden, his opponent, who should have been President, had been a demagogue or a man who wanted to start it, we would have had a civil war right then and there.

"But Hayes was a real statesman. Reversing his policy of the election campaign on becoming President, he called in the Southerners and told them that he would do what Tilden had proposed to do and that is: he would take the troops out of the South and give the southern states a chance to recover. He did just that, and you have got to give Hayes credit for that.

"Woodrow Wilson was the first one who realized the world position of the United States. Wilson tried to make a world power out of us. He was far ahead of his time. In fact, he was thirty-one years ahead of his time in his League of Nations proposal. Failure of the League was followed by war again.

"When Franklin Roosevelt met Winston Churchill in the Atlantic in August, 1941, the foreign policy of the United States was completely reversed. We had slipped into isolation after our rejection of the League and now Roosevelt has changed that.

"I have tried to implement that Roosevelt policy, because, whether we like it or not, we are the most powerful nation in the world today. We are trying to use the power we have for the welfare of the world, and not for its destruction.

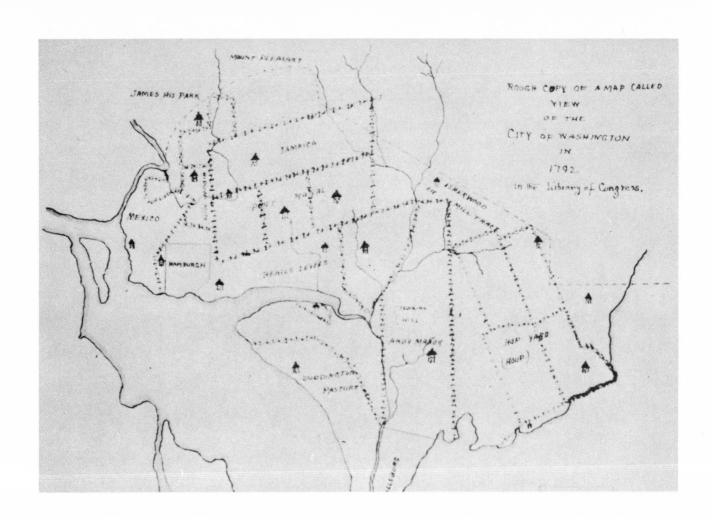

ROUGH COPY OF A MAP CALLED
VIEW
OF THE
CITY OF WASHINGTON
IN
1792.
In the Library of Congress.

One mile from Washington City Hall!

"You may be sure that we have no intention of overrunning our neighbors in Central America or in South America or to the north either by military means or by political means."

I asked Mr. Truman what presidents had difficulties which paralleled his.

The President said:

"Well, there was Andrew Johnson. He was trying to carry out the program of his predecessor, Abraham Lincoln, and he even got impeached while doing it. That is, I think, about the nearest to the case.

"Jackson had difficulty because he succeeded John Quincy Adams, and John Quincy Adams was elected as a Democrat—they called them Democrat-Republicans in those days —and Jackson was to reverse completely the financial policy of his predecessor, as you will remember. Jackson destroyed the Bank of the United States and put the finances of the government on an even keel. In fact, old Jackson led the country out of debt, but I am somewhat of the opinion that is what caused the panic of 1837.

"Lincoln had a good deal of difficulty with his Cabinet. One of the things about Lincoln that so endears him to everybody is the fact that he was just a common everyday citizen, was glad to admit it and act like one. But Lincoln had a whole lot of smart alecks in his Cabinet. They thought they knew a darn sight more than he did. They questioned the advisability of issuing the Emancipation Proclamation.

"Lincoln said: 'Well, there's only one deciding vote. The vote is aye.' "

Here President Truman turned to the subject of press attacks on him. I found that he had made a special study of the criticisms of all the presidents of the United States.

"Even George Washington was not exempt from some of the most vicious slanders," said Mr. Truman. "He was accused of wrongfully appropriating land belonging to a friend of his, and even of overdrawing his pay as President. As a matter of fact, the Father of our Country could not at first be persuaded to run for a second term, because he was so bitter over misrepresentations of his life and conduct in office.

"In going over the history of various presidents I find that this is nothing new. There never was a more thoroughly misrepresented man than Thomas Jefferson. Of course, you are familiar with how they treated Andrew Jackson. Following him the two most thoroughly misrepresented were Grover Cleveland and Woodrow Wilson. They almost hounded Cleveland to his grave. It is interesting to read the lies they published about him and Mrs. Cleveland.

"Lincoln, of course, was thoroughly misrepresented and it took fifty years to get at the

GROVER CLEVELAND

truth. So I don't let these things bother me for the simple reason I know that I am trying to do the right thing and eventually the facts will come out.

"I'll probably be holding a conference with Saint Peter when that happens.

"I never give much weight or attention to the brickbats that are thrown my way. The people that cause me concern are the good men who have to take these brickbats for me.

"I can't help what they say about me because most of it has been said before, but it does make it very difficult for the government to obtain men of ability, who generally refuse to be targets.

"You ask for some parallels in American history to the situation which I face.

"Not long ago I wrote a friend of mine that I had received a cartoon from the London *Punch* which showed a Carthaginian senator making a speech—'What! Let Hannibal use the elephant on his own initiative?'

"It is this attitude that kept Hannibal from winning the Second Punic War. There are innumerable instances parallel to what has happened in the Carthaginian Senate.

"Jefferson's decision to wipe out the Barbary pirates caused almost as much denunciation as my decision to implement the Atlantic Treaty—so conditions do not change.

"But when all is said and done and history is written people never remember the men who tried to obstruct what was necessary to be done. I don't think anybody ever remem-

bers the names of men who attacked Washington on account of the Jay Treaty, nor do they remember the attackers who vilified Jefferson for making the Louisiana Purchase. They almost brought impeachment charges against him.

"Let me repeat, there never was a man as completely vilified as Lincoln when he took the reins in his own hands and called for 75,000 volunteers to meet the secession of the southern states. The same thing is true of Grover Cleveland in his ultimatum to England over the Venezuela boundary.

"The editorial writers jumped on Wilson for sending Funston into Veracruz and Pershing into northern Mexico. I don't think anybody remembers the attacks any more than they will remember those of the present day.

"It is the business of the President to meet situations as they arise and to meet them in the public interest.

"Our American political situation is about the same from generation to generation. The main difficulty is that the rising generation never knows about the acts of the previous one —most people think it too much trouble to find out."

I reminded the President that when he was chairman of the famous Truman Committee to investigate the national defense program at the beginning of the second world war that he had taken the trouble to find out what had been done by previous similar Congressional committees.

The President said:

"Yes, I made it a point to get out the records of the 'Joint Committee of Congress to Inquire into the Management of the Civil War,' or the War Between the States. As I wrote to Wayne Grover, head of the National Archives in Washington, the committee of which I was chairman was lucky enough not to make the same mistakes that were made by Senator Wade and Congressman Gooch and others who proved to be a handicap to President Lincoln.

"After President Roosevelt discovered that the objective of the committee was to contribute something to the winning of the war he gave me his wholehearted cooperation. Of course, as a result of the successful operation I succeeded in getting myself into more trouble than any man ever inherited." (Becoming President.)

"We profited to some extent by our experiences after World War 1.

"I find that our problems are almost parallel with those after the Revolutionary War and with those which took place after Andrew Jackson's administration which ended in the late thirties. They are also similar to those we faced after World War 1, too.

"I am as confident as I can be that if strong men had been in the White House from 1850 to 1860 the bloody war which started in 1861 could have been avoided or at least indefinitely postponed.

"We are faced with the same condition with which the country was faced from 1850 to 1860 only on a world-wide basis and I am certainly hoping that we can arrive at a conclusion that will not end in total destruction of civilization.

"The troubles of the human race cannot be solved if man thinks only of bread and butter, meat and shoes and fancy clothes. Cultural activities are absolutely necessary to get the minds of men slanted for the welfare of the race."

I asked the President what other Americans, besides presidents, had interested him or even influenced him.

He replied: "I have always been very much interested in Seward, who negotiated the cession of Alaska. Next to Jefferson and Polk, he made the most important acquisition of territory for the country.

"Lincoln made him Secretary of State, and a clique tried to force him out, but Lincoln wouldn't budge.

"He served all through Lincoln's administration and that of Andrew Johnson as Secretary of State and he was a good Secretary of State. He helped keep England from recognizing the Confederacy.

"Franklin is a man who is worth studying. He was a compromiser. If it had not been for him there wouldn't have been any Constitution. He knew how to handle men and get them to agree. He helped Washington who was presiding officer of the Constitutional Convention in a way that made the Convention a success. Franklin was the author of 'We must all hang together, or assuredly we shall all hang separately.' I don't think Franklin has ever found his real place in history yet—he was one of the great ones of his time and of all American history."

III

As the President went on talking about American history, I interrupted to ask what he understood by the term "the American way of life." The President said:

"The ideal of the American way of life may be summed up in the Bill of Rights and the idea that there ought to be equality of opportunity for everybody to make a living. Every man has a right to make a living and then it is up to him to make good.

"Most Americans want to own their own house and lot, or a small farm, and then raise a family. The children are usually brought up under three influences: first, the mother, who has the greatest influence of anybody; then the Sunday school teacher and then the school teacher. They help make American character. And that is founded on the fundamental idea of giving everybody an education."

IV

I once heard the President say that politics was like military tactics. I asked him to explain.

Mr. Truman said:

"The maneuvers in a battle are like the maneuvers in politics. In the military they have what they call a five paragraph order.

"In the first paragraph you make an estimate of the enemy, his condition and what he can do.

"In the second paragraph, you make an estimate of your own condition and what *you* can do.

"In the third paragraph you decide what you are *going* to do.

"The fourth paragraph—you set up your logistics and supply sources to *carry out* what you are going to do.

"And in the fifth paragraph, you tell *where* you are going to be so that everybody can reach you.

"That is all there is to politics."

I asked the President if that was the reason he was interested in military affairs.

The President replied:

"No, not for that reason alone. Wars and military events have affected men so much. I'm afraid and I keep repeating it that even today men have not learned that the globe is too small for anybody to think they can run wild over it. That's why you still have to have the military.

"Many of the rulers of the world have been involved in fighting and you can't know your history without studying wars and military leaders.

"Take the Father of our Country. George Washington was not, in the estimate of some, a really great maneuver general."

I then asked the President what he thought of Washington as a military man.

"Well," Mr. Truman said, "he had the great ability to hold the morale of the people. In spite of all the conspiracies against him, including the Conway Cabal, and Gates, and Major André, he finally won the war and held the country together. He served as presiding

THE DECLARATION OF INDEPENDENCE

Key to Personages

1. Robert Morris . . . . *Pennsylvania*
2. Samuel Chase . . . . *Maryland*
3. Charles Carroll of Carrollton . . . . *Maryland*
4. Stephen Hopkins . . . . . . *Rhode Island*
5. Samuel Adams . . . . . . *Massachusetts*
6. Thomas McKean . . . . *Delaware*
7. John Dickinson . . . . *Pennsylvania*
8. Abraham Clark . . . . *New Jersey*
9. William Ellery . . . . *Rhode Island*
10. John Witherspoon . . . . . . *New Jersey*
11. John Hancock . . . . *Massachusetts*
12. Benjamin Harrison . . . . *Virginia*
13. Samuel Huntington . . . . . . *Connecticut*
14. Thomas Jefferson . . . . *Virginia*
15. Roger Sherman . . . . *Connecticut*
16. John Adams . . . . *Massachusetts*
17. Robert R. Livingston . . . . . . *New York*
18. Benjamin Franklin . . . . . . *Pennsylvania*
19. Richard Henry Lee . . . . *Virginia*
20. Thomas Nelson, Jr. . . . . *Virginia*
21. Joseph Hewes . . . . *North Carolina*
22. Edward Rutledge . . . . . *South Carolina*
23. Lyman Hall . . . . *Georgia*
24. Josiah Bartlett . . . . *New Hampshire*
25. Thomas Stone . . . . *Maryland*
26. Francis Hopkinson . . . . . . *New Jersey*
27. George Wythe . . . . *Virginia*
28. William Floyd . . . . *New York*

THE MURALS BY BARRY FAULKNER

officer for the Constitutional Convention and that is the reason we have a Constitution, that and the fact he could get along with this old man Benjamin Franklin."

The President went on talking of military men.

"Old Jackson at the battle of New Orleans was our next outstanding general. That

20 21   22   23 24   25

1 2 3   4   5   6   7 8 9 10 11   12 13 14   15   16   17   18   19

THE CONSTITUTION OF THE UNITED STATES

Key to Personages

1. Edmund Randolph . . . . *Virginia*
2. Nathaniel Gorham . . . . . . *Massachusetts*
3. John Dickinson . . . . *Delaware*
4. John Rutledge . . . . . . *South Carolina*
5. James Wilson . . . . *Pennsylvania*
6. Oliver Ellsworth . . . . *Connecticut*
7. Charles Pinckney . . . . . *South Carolina*
8. James Madison . . . . *Virginia*
9. Elbridge Gerry . . . . *Massachusetts*
10. William Samuel Johnson . . . . *Connecticut*
11. George Mason . . . . *Virginia*
12. George Washington . . . . . . *Virginia*
13. Benjamin Franklin . . . . . . *Pennsylvania*

14. Rufus King . . . . *Massachusetts*
15. William Paterson . . . . . . *New Jersey*
16. Charles Cotesworth Pinckney . . *South Carolina*
17. Gouverneur Morris . . . . . . *Pennsylvania*
18. Alexander Hamilton . . . . *New York*
19. George Read . . . . *Delaware*
20. William R. Davie . . . . . *North Carolina*
21. John Langdon . . . . . . *New Hampshire*
22. Luther Martin . . . . *Maryland*
23. Roger Sherman . . . . *Connecticut*
24. Gunning Bedford, Jr. . . . . . . *Delaware*
25. Abraham Baldwin . . . . *Georgia*

IN THE NATIONAL ARCHIVES

battle made him President, although the battle was fought days after the war was over, because at that time there were no swift communications.

"And then there was Zachary Taylor who was in the war with Mexico. He was, I think, one of the best military leaders of that time. I don't know what he would have done as President if he had lived long enough.

"Of course, the greatest of all in Lincoln's day was Robert E. Lee. Lee was a great tactician and leader in the field. Yet when the surrender came, he became president of

what is now called Washington and Lee University—the name Lee was not added until after his death—and he made as important a contribution to the rehabilitation of the country as anybody in that day. If you will look into the details of his presidency at Washington and Lee, you will find that he knew every boy in that school.

"He was interested in the welfare of all the boys and some of the letters he wrote by hand to the parents of those kids are 'out of this world.' Which shows that he was not only great as a military man but that he had the right idea of what the next generation ought to learn and how it ought to act.

"There were great generals on the other side of the fence, too. Grant, of course, by his bulldog persistence finally wound up the war.

"Sheridan was a fine cavalry leader and his opposite number on the other side was Jeb Stuart. If he were alive today we would call Jeb Stuart a publicity hound. He was a great cavalry leader, although he caused Lee to lose the battle of Gettysburg—which was a drawn battle, I think.

"He had gone off on a trip of his own, and as Lee marched up from the Shenandoah Valley to Cashtown Pass west of Gettysburg he had no communication with Stuart at all. Stuart arrived on the first day of the Battle of Gettysburg. Lee's only comment was: 'Well, General Stuart, you are here at last.'

"That was a gentle comment but from a man like Lee it was terrific. He never scolded anybody at all. Longstreet and Jackson couldn't get along. Longstreet had the First Corps and Jackson the Second Corps. At the battle of Fredericksburg, Longstreet and Jackson had a fuss. Lee stood it as long as he could. And he said, 'You are all fighting each other, we ought to be fighting the enemy.' That ended it.

"Let me tell you about a fellow who never got his dues, and that is a fat man who was commanding general in the Spanish-American War—Major General W. R. Shafter. He was six feet four inches tall, and weighed three hundred pounds. He was so fat he couldn't ride a horse. He used a buckboard at the battle of Santiago. He got unjustly abused because of the tainted meat scandal at the time, but he moved 20,000 men from Tampa, Florida, to the point of contact successfully, and won the battle."

The President began talking about Sherman.

"You know," he said, "Sherman was supposed to have said, 'War is hell.' Well, that's right whoever said it. And Sherman, who was a great military leader, created enough hell as he went along. Sherman's attack on the breadbasket and munitions center of the Confederacy is really what defeated them because when he marched and took Atlanta and went down to the sea, that cut the Confederacy squarely in two.

"There was a remarkable southern general who started as a private at forty-one years of age and ended up as a lieutenant general when the war was over. He was Nathan Bedford Forrest and he could hardly read or write. One of his lieutenants asked for a leave, and he wrote an endorsement on his request for leave, 'i tole you twicit goddamit no.' Forrest headed the Ku Klux Klan after the war, but he broke it up when he found it had gone bad."

The President said that one thing all great generals had in common:

"They were brave and they were not afraid to go up in the front line with the men when it was necessary.

"I think the greatest general in all history is Hannibal. Hannibal, the Carthaginian, licked Spain with an army that I don't think had over thirty to forty thousand men in it. He then marched over the Alps into Italy. He fought in Italy without home support for sixteen years and he never lost a battle. You compare that if you can. The merchants of Carthage caused their own destruction because they would not support him.

"If the merchants of Carthage had, there would have been no Rome. Maybe the world is better off that the merchants didn't support him.

"Hannibal was finally defeated when the Carthaginians sent for him after the Roman Scipio Africanus had landed in Carthage in the Second Punic War. They gave him an untrained army and he lost the critical battle. He had to flee. He went to the court of Prusias, King of Bithynia. When the Romans demanded of Prusias to turn him over to them Hannibal chose suicide. The only records we have of Hannibal are written by his enemies. There is no Carthaginian history because Carthage was completely destroyed. Everything we know about him is told to us by the Romans. Despite that he still stands out as the greatest of them all. He had only one eye. He lost one of his eyes when he was eighteen years old in Spain.

"I guess the next greatest general is Alexander. Alexander's greatest battle was a perfect maneuver battle like Chancellorsville, centuries later. It resulted in a complete victory with only about a third the number of the troops the enemy had.

"Of course in modern times the greatest of them is Napoleon. The battle of Austerlitz is another perfect maneuver.

"As a matter of fact most of the battles in our Civil War were battles of maneuver. That is why officers of European army staffs have for years come to this country to study the Civil War battlegrounds and history.

"The first world war in 1914 got away from the maneuvers except for Hindenburg's defeat of the Russians at the Masurian Lakes or the Battle of Tannenburg. Hindenburg had been a student of the tactics and strategy of Robert E. Lee.

"I think of our able modern field generals, Bradley tops them all. He had more men under his command in the field than any other general in the history of the world.

RALLY OF THE TROOPS AT WASHINGTON

"Bradley's march to Berlin is one of the great maneuvers of the world. Bradley is one of the most unassuming men you ever met. There never was a finer man, and he is smart."

The President said if he had time he could go on talking for hours about the outstanding generals of history.

"You know," said the President, "great leaders have had something, that special quality, which distinguished them from others. Napoleon had something that all great leaders had. The best illustration of that something is when he came back from Elba. Marshal Ney was the commanding general for King Louis the Eighteenth. Ney told Louis he would bring Napoleon back in an iron cage, and Ney then went down to meet him at the gate. When Napoleon got out of his carriage and turned to Ney, Napoleon said, 'My great marshal.'

"So strong was Napoleon's magnetism that Ney abandoned the king and joined Napoleon. A fellow has got to have something to be able to do that."

V

The President one day voiced a startling criticism of Charles Dickens.

He blames this famous novelist for being responsible—innocently of course—for dimming the luster of one of the great Biblical names—Uriah.

"One of the bravest and one of the best soldiers was Uriah," the President said. "But the quality of the name of Uriah has been ruined because Charles Dickens created a character named Uriah Heep, a sniveling hypocrite. Charles Dickens shouldn't have used that name which is a name of a man of bravery and daring, the name of a man who would not stay at home with his people because his men were in the field and he didn't think he ought to enjoy himself if his men could not."

The President's knowledge of the Bible and Biblical stories is as rich in detail and in observation as that of politics and military things. Even in this field the President finds men who are not properly appreciated.

"Take Amos," says the President. "He is one of the minor prophets and he is not often talked or preached about. There are only nine chapters in the Bible on Amos but Amos says as much in those few chapters as Isaiah did in sixty-six chapters. Amos was interested in the welfare of the average man. That is what the prophets were, they were the protagonists of the common man, and that is the reason they survived, and for no other reason. Every one of these prophets were trying to help the underdog, and the greatest prophet was crucified because He was trying to help the underdog."

In his study at Blair House one evening he opened the Bible at random, saying:

"You can open the Bible accidentally and come up with something interesting. What have we here?

" 'O Lord, what shall I say when Israel turneth their backs before their enemies?'

"That was Joshua speaking. He was another fighting man, you know. And we have got people that turn their backs before the enemy today.

"I was reading the other night the sorrowful verse of the twelfth chapter of Ecclesiastes that makes you sit up and take notice: 'Vanity of vanities . . . all is vanity.' "

I asked him what other passages in the Bible he liked, and he said:

"I think some of the passages in Jeremiah and Daniel are wonderful. I like the Proverbs and the Psalms—the 137th Psalm, 'By the rivers of Babylon,' of course, is the famous one, and the 96th, 'O, sing unto the Lord a new song.' They are wonderful, they are just like poetry. And read the passages in Deuteronomy that are seldom referred to. The Ten Commandments are repeated in Deuteronomy in sonorous language that really makes a tingle go down your spine to read them.

"Of course the Sermon on the Mount is the greatest of all things in the Bible, a way of life, and maybe some day men will get to understand it as the real way of life."

The fundamental facts of this Nation's law was given to Moses on the Mount.

H.S.T.

It was natural here for us to talk about morals and ethical standards. I asked President Truman what his idea of a moral code was. He was refreshing and interesting in his comments, and the following morning he handed me a four-page handwritten memorandum on White House stationery, summarizing his views.

It read:

"A moral code is one based on proper relations with other people and on a faith in the religious concept of a future after the life on earth.

"Egypt, Mesopotamia, Greece, Rome all had such moral codes.

"Ours comes from ancient Israel and the Sermon on the Mount.

"Buddha, Confucius and other great Oriental teachers had almost the same sort of ethical view of life and how to live happily with our fellow men.

"The basis of all great moral codes is 'Do to and for others what you would have others do to and for yourself.'

"Treat others as you would like to be treated.

"Truth, honor and justice are at the basis of all human relations. No really great man in history but had these attributes.

"There have been great military leaders who had none of these fundamental qualifications. Most of them came to a bad end. But those great statesmen and military leaders who had the moral qualifications named made a contribution to the welfare and advancement of the world.

"Great teachers like Moses, Isaiah, Confucius, Buddha, Mohammed, Saint Thomas Aquinas, Martin Luther, John Knox and many others were imbued with honor, truth and justice.

"Jefferson, I think, is the greatest ethical teacher of our time. He was unusual in that he was able, as Governor of Virginia, member of the Continental Congress and President of the United States, to put his teachings into practice.

"In ancient times, Jesus Christ was the greatest teacher of them all—not only ancient but modern."

PART THREE

Diaries, Private Memoranda, Papers

I

President Truman made available to me his diaries, private memoranda and papers. Those portions published here illustrate what goes on in the mind of a President and the manner of man he is, but are not a complete record. President Truman does not always keep a day-to-day account of his thoughts and actions. He is no Pepys.

But once a week, or oftener when a situation warrants it, the President writes a memorandum in longhand, outlining facts, decisions and the persons involved with his plain-speaking comments.

The President keeps his diaries in black leather notebooks. But his memoranda are written on blocks of paper, five by eight, and none of them have been type-copied or designed in any way for any eyes but his.

The President told me that the writing of these memoranda helps him to clarify his thinking and serve as notes for further study and decision.

For the first year of his Presidency, Mr. Truman penciled brief but pungent comments on the margin of his daily appointments sheet. For example, after listening to one visitor for fifteen minutes, the President wrote simply: "Baloney peddler." Or having discussed the international situation with a public figure, he recorded in pencil: "This man not only wants to run the country but the universe and the entire milky way." On the margin of his visitors' list of March 23, 1946, after the following item for 10.00 A.M. (General Walter Bedell Smith, U. S. Ambassador to Russia), the President writes in longhand in ink: "Told him to tell Stalin I held him to be a man to keep his word. Troops in Iran after March 2, upset that theory. Also told him to urge Stalin to come to U.S.A." 7.10 P.M. (Leave for Mayflower Hotel to attend Jackson Day Dinner): "An enthusiastic meeting. My first political speech as President. Rang the bell, I believe."

Running throughout the diaries and private papers, one theme predominates: "I don't want this Republic to go the way of the Greek and Roman republics. If we can keep the responsibility in the civil population, it won't. When you get a mercenary military setup, then the Republic has gone, and you finally end up with a man on horseback. I am going to turn over the government to civilians who are in complete control, and I hope they will follow through on it."

The President is a man of fervid convictions and the diary mirrors his thoughts and concern about public issues which he advocates. But I was not surprised to find written passages of beauty and gentle irony. Every now and then with boisterous humor he writes "Ain't that sompin"; as for example in recording that a wealthy man had received a Communist decoration. And the President never ceases to observe and to record the awe in which the people hold the Presidency.

The President said: "No matter how much the man who sits here may be properly criticized, I hope the critics will once in a while remember that he is the President of the United States as well as a human being."

The diaries and private papers reveal a devout man broad in his aims, stern in his purpose, firm in his loyalties yet serene about the future.

II

The first notes recorded by the President in the White House were in pencil, as follows:

April 13.   Signed Proclamation for Pres. R's funeral and holiday. First official act.
            Saw Sec. State. Approved communication to P.M. of G.B.
            Saw Jim Byrnes.
            Lunch with the Senate and House leaders. Saw *all* the Senators.
            Most overcome by treatment.
            Agreed to joint session to be announced by Legislative leaders.
            Afternoon saw Byrnes, Roy Roberts, Duke Shoop for social visit.
            Saw Sec. State on wire to Churchill and one to Stalin.

Sat.   John Snyder, Fulton, Byrnes, Ed McKim came in.
            Had Henry Wallace and Byrnes ride with me to station.

April 18.   Session with State, War, Navy on Trusteeships. Authorized agreement in it
            for San Francisco.
            Authorized State, War and Navy to confer on matters affecting political and
            military problems in the war areas.. (*Hadn't been done before.*)
            Mr. Early, Mr. Hassett, and Mr. Daniels, Judge Rosenman have offered to
            stay and help me get things organized for which I'm very grateful.

*Several days later, the President found time to fill in the more complete details of those
first days, and then to begin his diary entries:*

April 12, 1945

At 3:35 P.M. I was presiding over Senate. Senate adjourned about five o'clock and Sam
Rayburn called me up and asked me if I could stop off at his office—some legislative matters about which he wanted to talk. I arrived at Rayburn's office about 5:05 and there
was a call from Steve Early, asking me to come to the White House as quickly as possible.
I told Sam Rayburn and some Congressmen, who were present, to say nothing about it;

I would probably be back in a few minutes, expecting probably I was going to see the President because Bishop Atwood was to be buried that day; and I thought maybe the President was in town for the funeral and wanted to go over some matter with me before returning to Warm Springs.

Before going I went to my office, got my hat. Tom Harty drove me up to the White House. Arrived there about 5:25 P.M. and was ushered into Mrs. Roosevelt's study on second floor.

Mrs. Roosevelt and Steve Early and Colonel and Mrs. Boettiger were there. Mrs. Roosevelt put her arm around my shoulder and said, "The President is dead." That was the first inkling I had of the seriousness of the situation.

I then asked them what I could do, and she said, "What can we do for you?" Before I had a chance to say anything, Secretary of State Stettinius came in. He evidently had received the news, because he was in tears.

I decided to call a meeting of the Cabinet to take place as quickly as possible in regular cabinet room. I left Mrs. Roosevelt's study, and Colonel Boettiger went to cabinet room with me. Telephoned to Les Biffle, Secretary of Senate, who came over immediately. Attorney General came in, and other members of the Cabinet were telephoned. As soon as I went to the cabinet room, Early released the news that the President had died that afternoon. Cabinet assembled and in the meantime, I had telephoned Chief Justice Harlan F. Stone, to come as quickly as possible and I sent a car for my wife and daughter. Had both floor leaders of the House, and the floor leader of the Senate, majority and minority leaders of the Senate, and President pro tempore of the Senate telephoned. Some of them arrived and some did not. As soon as my wife and daughter arrived, which was about 7 o'clock, an effort was made to find a Bible on which to take the oath. Found Bible which belonged in a White House bookcase and Chief Justice Stone administered oath, beginning at 7:08 and finished at 7:09. I immediately called a meeting of the Cabinet and asked all of the members to remain in office.

Mr. Stettinius asked me if I wanted the San Francisco Conference to go on, and I said the San Francisco Conference should be held as directed by the President.

Mrs. Roosevelt then asked me if it would be all right for her and family to take a plane to go to Warm Springs, and I told her she could have anything the Government had to use in any way she saw fit. They left about a half hour after Cabinet meeting adjourned, and I went on home to my apartment at 4701 Connecticut Avenue.

I was very much shocked. I am not easily shocked but was certainly shocked when I was told of the President's death and the weight of the Government had fallen on my shoulders. I did not know what reaction the country would have to the death of a man whom they all practically worshipped. I was worried about reaction of the Armed Forces. I did not know what effect the situation would have on the war effort, price control, war production and everything. I knew the President had a great many meetings with Churchill and Stalin. I was not familiar with any of these things, and it was really something to think about but I decided the best thing to do was to go home and get as much rest as possible and face the music.

My wife and daughter and mother-in-law were at the apartment of our next door neighbor and their daughter, Mrs. Irving Wright, was present. They had had a turkey dinner and they gave us something to eat. I had not had anything to eat since noon. Went to bed, went to sleep, and did not worry any more that day.

Next morning the Secret Service came out as usual—they had been coming after me every morning. They took me down the back way, and I got in the car. I saw Tony Vaccaro. I hailed him—had him get in the car and ride down with me. Went to the White House office and began the day. Hugh Fulton came to the house that morning and he also came down with me in the car. Ed McKim was not at home—he was in town.

10:15   The Secretary of State, General George C. Marshall, Admiral Ernest J. King, Admiral William D. Leahy, the Secretary of War, the Secretary of the Navy, and General Giles. Discussed the best way to get word to the troops what the new Commander in Chief expected to do. I told them I thought the first thing I would do would be to appear before the Congress and make a statement and then make a statement immediately after that to the soldiers in the field, and they agreed that a good procedure.

12:00   That day at noon Admiral Wilson Brown, Naval Aide here, Colonel Richard Park and Jonathan Daniels called and discussed foreign dispatches.

12:30   Went up to Capitol—had lunch and discussed with the members of the Senate and some members of the House advisability of a message on Monday—some of them opposed it. I listened to what all had to say. Then I said, I am coming and prepare for me. I thought it was the proper thing to do. They finally came around to my way of thinking when they found out what I had in mind—a statement of continuing the policies of the late President, outlining the war effort and asking their cooperation.

The following were present at the luncheon:

THE PRESIDENT

SENATOR BARKLEY	SENATOR WHITE	MR. RAMSPECK
MR. MCCORMACK	MR. RAYBURN	SENATOR CONNALLY
SENATOR HILL	MR. MARTIN	SENATOR AUSTIN
SENATOR MAGNUSON	SENATOR VANDENBERG	SENATOR LA FOLLETTE
SENATOR PEPPER	SENATOR GEORGE	SENATOR HATCH
MR. BIFFLE (host)	SENATOR O'MAHONEY	SENATOR WHEELER

2:30   James F. Byrnes called. I found out Jimmie was at Shoreham Hotel—called up and asked him to come over. We discussed everything from Teheran to Yalta. Message from Stalin came in—said he would like to do anything he could to cooperate and I immediately sent him message back—copy of message on file in Leahy's office.

3:30   The Secretary of State and Charles Bohlen called. Discussed Molotov. Stalin wired he was sending Molotov. Discussed matter with Stettinius before I sent wire in reply to Stalin.

April 14, 1945

9:00   Saw John Snyder. Asked him to be Federal Loan Administrator—he did not want to do it—said he did not think he was right man for the place. Jimmie Byrnes came in a little while after that and I told him I was going to make John Snyder Federal Loan Administrator, and he said that was the best pick I could make. Then I called Walter Smith, President of the Bank, told him I wanted John Snyder for Loan Administrator. Smith said he hated to lose him but if I wanted him, I could have him. In a day or two after that, I sent John Snyder's name to Senate—called up Jesse Jones and told him the President had made the appointment and he said—did he make that appointment before he died and I said no—HE made it just now.

9:15   Secretary of Treasury wanted to discuss some financing arrangements. Said he would do anything in the world to cooperate.

9:45   Left for Union Station to meet the President's funeral train. Took Wallace and Byrnes in car with me. Went to station and as soon as train pulled in we got aboard—met all the Roosevelt family and then followed the procession—came back to office.

11:30   Harry Hopkins came in.

12:30   Had lunch at desk with Harry Hopkins and discussed the whole history of the Roosevelt administration 1933 to date—particularly emphasis on the foreign visit on which the President had taken Harry Hopkins. We discussed Stalin, Churchill, De Gaulle, Cairo, Casablanca, Teheran and Yalta.

2:15   Admiral Leahy—talked regarding messages passing back and forth from Churchill and Stalin.

4:00   Attended funeral service in the White House. Went out to apartment after funeral. Ten o'clock that night left for Hyde Park.

April 15

We arrived at Hyde Park about 9:30 in the morning and waited for the funeral procession to be organized. Went up to Hyde Park burial lot where the most impressive ceremony took place, and the President was buried. Mrs. Roosevelt told me she would like to finish some work at the White House. I told her to do anything she wanted to do, and to take her time. We left about 12 o'clock. I saw a great many people on train going up or coming back. That afternoon we worked on the address I proposed to make to Congress the next day. We had outlined it going up. Mrs. Roosevelt called on me and some of the Roosevelt children. I saw a great many Senators and members of the House who were at the funeral. They came to the train to pay their respects. We worked all afternoon on address to Congress.

On visit down to Senate I saw all the Senators who were present that day; in addition saw Senate pages, employees of the Senate, all members of Senate press gallery, told newspapermen if they ever prayed, which I very much doubted, that they had better pray for me now.

Coming from funeral train—old and young were crying on the streets—old Negro woman sitting down on curb with apron on was crying like she had lost her son. Most of the women and half the men in tears on Constitution Avenue when coming back from meeting funeral train. I shall never forget the scene. The reaction of the people moved me. I was moved by what my Mother said. Statement my Mother gave out was a jewel. If it had been prepared by the best public relations man it could not have been better. My Mother said, "I cannot really be glad my son is President because I am sorry that President Roosevelt is dead. If he had been voted in, I would be out waving a flag, but it does not seem right to be very happy or wave any flags now. Harry will get along. I knew Harry would be all right after I heard him give his speech this morning. I heard every word of it but Mary, my daughter, is going to read it to me. Everyone who heard him talk this morning will know he is sincere and will do what is best."

On May 12, 1945, he began one of his early memoranda:

The courts, I think, should be strictly judicial and not dabble in policy—except interpretation of the Constitution. It is not at all proper for courts to try to make laws or to read law school theories into the law and policy as laid down by the Congress. We want no Gestapo or Secret Police. . . . I should like to see the Constitution amended to do away with all two-thirds rules. This means treaty ratification and presidential vetoes. These two matters should be accomplished by requiring a majority of those present. Every legislator should be required to express his opinion by vote on these two most important legislative responsibilities. They should never be accomplished by unanimous consent. Impeachment should be made simpler. And an impeachment court should be set up or the Supreme Court should conduct the trial. The result to be ratified by a majority of Senate and House— same sort of majority as before stated. School system needs overhauling. Kids should learn more fundamental "reading, writing and arithmetic."

May 22, 1945

Had a long talk with Joe Davies last night on the Russian situation. Had previously discussed it with him on May 13. He suggested a cable by him to Molotov for Stalin in which he suggested a meeting of Stalin and myself in Alaska or Siberia or on a warship somewhere in that neighborhood.

He had come over to tell me how blue he was over our deteriorating relations with Russia.

I informed him that at Harriman's suggestion and after a consultation with Hull, Byrnes

and others, I had sent Harry Hopkins to see Stalin with instructions to tell Stalin my views and that I would be pleased to meet him face to face.

Told Davies I had sent Hopkins because I trusted him and because he had been Roosevelt's messenger to Russia on a previous and similar occasion, that Hopkins was a noted and advanced "Liberal" but not a professional one (I consider the latter a low form of politician), that he had horse sense and knew how to use it.

I had previously suggested to Davies on May 13th that he go but his health would not allow it. Anyway, as it worked out Hopkins is the best bet from our standpoint. Davies suggested that if he could talk with Churchill he could make him see the light. He thought Churchill had been importuning me to urge Stalin to come to a meeting. But Churchill wanted me to meet with him first—which I do not want to do. Stalin already has an erroneous opinion we are ganging up on him.

To have a reasonably lasting peace, the three great powers must be able to trust each other, and they must themselves honestly want it. They must also have the confidence of the *smaller* nations. . . . I want peace and I am willing to work hard for it. It is my opinion we will get it.

I suggested to Davies, after he said he could talk to Churchill, that he go and do it—if his physical condition would stand it. . . . Davies said he would go to London.

So I have sent Hopkins to Moscow and Davies to London. We shall see what we shall see. . . .

I told Hopkins what I had in mind. He said he would go, said he understood my position and that he would make it clear to Uncle Joe Stalin that I knew what I wanted—and that I intended to get it—peace for the world for at least 90 years. That we have no territorial ambitions or ulterior motives in Poland, Rumania, Bulgaria, Czechoslovakia, Austria, Yugoslavia, Latvia, Lithuania, Estonia, or elsewhere, and that our only interests concern world peace. . . .

Stettinius came to see me from San Francisco and asked me to make certain decisions on controversial matters now pending at the Conference. I made them in red pencil and gave him the copy. Told him I would come out to San Francisco and close the conference. He sent me photostat copies of my own red penciled markings on his copy of the suggestions.

Evidently, some of the State Department boys believe nobody not even the President of the United States. Ain't it awful? Must make changes.

I've no faith in any totalitarian state. . . . They all start with a wrong premise—that lies are justified and that the old disproven formula that the end justifies the means is right and necessary to maintain the power of government.

I do not agree, and I do not believe that such methods can help humanity toward the long-hoped-for millennium. . . .

Anyway, the human animal cannot be trusted for anything *good* except en masse. The combined thought and action of the whole people of any race, creed or nationality, will always point in the right direction. "As you would others should do unto you, do ye also unto them." Confucius, Buddha, Christ and all moralists come to the same conclusion.

May 27, 1945

My daughter and her two pals, Jane Lingo and Mrs. Wright—both lovely kids, are sleeping in Lincoln's bed tonight! If I were not afraid it would scare them too badly I would have Lincoln appear. The maids and butlers swear he has appeared on several occasions. It is said that even Mrs. Coolidge saw him.

We had a picture show tonight: Jeanette MacDonald in "Springtime." Everybody, including me, cried a little—so we all enjoyed the show.

June 1, 1945

Yesterday was "medal pinning day," with one spilling over into this morning.

Gave Steve Early a Distinguished Service Medal. He's earned one in the last thirty days—let alone the previous twelve years.

Called all the White House force into the Rose Garden, read the citation and pinned the medal on him. Early said it was his mother's birthday, and both of us got sort of emotional. . . . In the morning I had given Mrs. Knox a Legion of Merit badge for the dead Secretary of the Navy. It was a nice ceremony, too, in the executive office with Secretaries of War and Navy present with their aides and assistants and wives. Mrs. Hull was present. . . .

Have been going through some very hectic days. Eyes troubling me somewhat. Too much reading "fine print." Nearly every memorandum has a catch in it, and it has been necessary to read at least a thousand of them and as many reports.

Most of it at night. I see the Secretaries at 9:15 after dictating personal mail for 45 minutes. Usually stop in the Map Room at 8:20 and inquire about ship sinkings, casualties, etc. Read dispatches from Stalin, Churchill, Hurley and others.

After discussing the day's prospects (schedule) with Connelly, Ross, Hassett, McKim and Early (I'll miss him) then commence to see the "customers."

Saw Herbert Hoover and had a pleasant and constructive conversation on food and the general troubles of U. S. presidents—two in particular.

We discussed our prima donnas and wondered what makes them. Some of my boys who came in with me are having trouble with their dignity and prerogatives. It's hell when a man gets in close association with the President. Something happens to him. Study Rienzi and one or two others.

Some Senators and Congressmen come in and pass the time of day and then go out and help me save the world in the press.

That publicity complex is hell and few can escape its lure. When a good man comes along who has not the bug I try to grab him.

The family left for Missouri last evening. Went to the train with them and rode to Silver Spring just as I did with my Mother and sister a week or so ago.

I am always so lonesome when the family leaves. I have no one to raise a fuss over my neckties and my haircuts, my shoes and my clothes generally. I usually put on a terrible tie which not even Bob Hannegan or Ed McKim would wear, just to get a loud protest from Bess and Margie.

When they are gone, I have to put on the right ones and it's no fun.

Went to church this morning and beat the publicity boys. Walked across . . . with no advance detail and slipped into a rear pew of —— Church without attracting any notice. Do not think over six people recognized me. Several soldiers and sailors stood and saluted me as I walked across the park but there were no curiosity seekers around and I enjoyed the lack of them.

Had dinner on the south porch all by myself. It is a beautiful outlook across the White House lawn to the Jefferson Memorial with the Washington Monument rising just to the left of the picture. And the Sabotage Press, represented by Mr. ——, did everything possible to prevent the building of the Jefferson Memorial. It makes a lovely picture from the south porch.

Church was rather dull. But I had a chance to do some thinking and the time was not wasted. A lot of the world's troubles have been caused by the interpretation of the Gospels and the controversies between sects and creeds. It is all so silly and comes of the prima donna complex again.

. . . I never thought God picked any favorites. It is my studied opinion that any race, creed or color can be God's favorites if they act the part and very few of them do that.

June 4, 1945

Some day. Alabama Senators and Representative Sparkman heard of a board vacancy and want it for Alabama. I admire their activity.

Saw the Big Four from Congress—McKellar, Barkley, Rayburn, McCormack. Rayburn spent weekend in Maryland at the fishing resort of ——. I was once taken to this resort on a

THE WHITE HOUSE
WASHINGTON

Saw Herbert Hoover day
before yesterday and had
a pleasant and constructive
conversation on food and
the general troubles of U.S.
Presidents — two in particular.

We discussed our prima
donnas and wondered what
makes 'em. Some of my boys
who came in with me are
having trouble with their
dignity and prerogatives. It's
hell when a man gets in
close association with the

THE WHITE HOUSE
WASHINGTON

President. Something happens
to him. Study Rienzi and
one or two others.

Some Senators and Con-
gressmen come in and
pass the time of day and then
go out and help me save
the world in the press.

That publicity complex is
hell and few can escape
its lure. When a good man
comes along who hasn't
the bug I try to get him

fishing trip before I became Vice President and they "accidentally" spilled me in the creek while I was changing seats in the row boat. I got wet from neck to ankles but kept my feet and head dry! Some feat. Try it sometime. I simply sat in the creek over the side of the boat, my feet stayed inside the boat and I held on to the side with my hands, keeping my head above the water. But I succeeded in getting just as wet as if I had gone all the way into the creek.

Can you imagine me now, taking sixteen Secret Service men, telephone and telegraph connections, representatives of three press associations, radio, photographers, and special writers on a personal excursion of that sort. And then let something like that happen. I will stay in the White House backyard and let them stare through the back fence at the "two-headed calf."

Joe Davies returned from his visit to the P.M. of Great Britain. Had him and Admiral Leahy to dinner and we discussed foreign affairs and Churchill in particular. After dinner a dozen or so Senators and the White House employees and their wives, sisters, cousins and aunts came to the East Room for a show by Olsen and Johnson. I took the show troupe over the House and told them what the President uses the Green, Blue, Red, and State Dining rooms for. Then took them upstairs and showed them where State guests sleep, the Lincoln and Monroe rooms and my own and the family quarters. I think they got a kick out of their high-powered guide—so did I.

June 5, 1945

Another hectic day in the executive office. Saw a lot of "customers." Hope they all left happy. Most of them did.

Took Ross, Snyder and Rosenman to the "House" for lunch. Had them upstairs in my so-called "study" before we went to the family dining room for lunch. Told the three of them that they were most in my confidence and that I wanted frank and unadulterated statements of facts to me from them—and that when they could not treat me on that basis, they would be of no use to me.

Went to a party this evening for Leslie Biffle. Max Truitt was the host. He is Barkley's son-in-law. I was a surprise guest. Arrived at the Hotel Raleigh lobby about seven o'clock. The Secret Service men were getting me through the lobby—pushing people right and left to make way for the President—politely—of course. We came to the elevator and there were Biffle, several Congressmen and a Senator or two waiting to go up. The Secret Service men who take care of the Nation's Chief Executive think only of the President and his convenience. Sometimes it is very embarrassing to a modest man. They began pushing Congressmen, Senators and other big shots out of the way at the elevator—even including the guest of honor—Mr. Biffle. Biffle is rather slight in build weighing about 130 pounds so

I grabbed him from behind by his elbows and shoved him into the elevator ahead of me. He thought he was being too roughly treated and turned on me to express his opinion. When he saw who was manhandling him, he was so surprised and happy that it made me ashamed.

The dinner was one great success. Truitt called on Biff's Senator from Arkansas, Bill Fulbright, who made some very appropriate remarks. Then he called on Judge Pike, Senator Scott Lucas, Senator Hatch, and his father-in-law, Senator Barkley. Barkley really spread himself. He not only paid a great tribute to Biffle but he went out of his way to pay a very high compliment to me.

Got back to the White House at 10:30. Called the Madam and talked to her and my baby girl (she does not like that designation). I cannot help wanting to talk to my sweetheart and my baby every night. I only had one sweetheart from the time I was six. I saw her in Sunday School at the Presbyterian Church in Independence, when my Mother took me there at that age, and afterwards in the fifth grade at the Ott School in Independence, when her Aunt Nannie was our teacher and she sat behind me. She sat behind me in the sixth, seventh and high school grades, and I thought she was the most beautiful and the sweetest person on earth—and I am still of that opinion after twenty-six years of being married to her. I am old-fashioned, I guess.

June 7, 1945

Looks like San Francisco may be a success yet. . . . We may get a peace yet. . . .

There's no Socialism in Russia. It is the hotbed of special privilege. A common everyday citizen has about as much to say about his government as an average stockholder in a giant corporation. But I do not care what they do. They evidently like their government or they would not die for it. I like ours, so let's get along. But when Russia puts out propaganda to help our parlor pinks—well that is bad—and that must stop. . . .

The United States was created by the boys and girls who could not get along at home. So-called Puritans, who were not by any manner of means pure, came to Massachusetts to try out their own witch-burning theories. Roger Williams could not stand them any better than he could stand England under the Stuarts. Most every colony on the East Coast was founded for about the same reason by folks who couldn't get along at home. But by amalgamation, we have made a very good country and a great nation with a reasonably good government. I want to maintain it, and shall do all I can in spite of the hyphenates and crackpots. I have no more use for any sort of hyphenates than I have for Communist Americans. They all have some other loyalty than the one they should have. Maybe the old melting pot will take care of it. I hope so.

June 13, 1945

Had breakfast with Hopkins, Davies and Leahy to discuss the Russian-British-Polish situation. . . . Propaganda seems to be our greatest foreign relations enemy. Russians distribute lies about us.

June 17, 1945

Went down the River today on the Potomac to discuss plans, issues and decisions. Took Charlie Ross, straight thinker, honest man, who tells me the truth so I understand what he means; Matt Connelly, shrewd Irishman, who raises up the chips (logs) and shows me bugs, honest, fair, "diplomatic" with me; Judge Fred Vinson, straight-shooter, knows Congress and how they think, a man to trust; Judge Rosenman, one of the ablest in Washington, keen mind, a lucid pen, a loyal Roosevelt man and equally loyal to me; Steve Early, a keen observer politically and otherwise.

We discussed public relations in Germany, Italy, France, Holland, Belgium, England and Russia. Food, fuel, transportation and what to do about it. Japanese War and the relations with China, Russia and Britain with regard to it.

July 4, 1945

Down Potomac on the Potomac with Vinson, Snyder, Rosenman, George Allen, Steve Early, Charlie Ross and Matt Connelly. Discussed Russia and Japanese war, government for Germany, *food,* fuel and transportation for Europe, sterling bloc. Do not feel happy over situation.

July 7, 1945
(On U.S.S. *Augusta,* enroute to Potsdam Conference.)

Had two rather full and interesting days. Received a committee of Congressmen and Senators who are members of the Lions Club. They presented me with an honorary membership, all framed, etc., and a scroll on principles of ethics. I said that business ethics would settle most trade difficulties and do away with courts of equity.

A couple of nice children gave me a plaque commemorating $715,000,000.00 on bond sales by the school children. The nice boy made me a speech. At his age, I would surely have passed out, if I had had to make a statement similar to his, to the town mayor, let alone the President of the United States. He did not seem to be much bothered or impressed. These modern kids are something to write home about, even if they cannot spell or find a word in the dictionary or tell what 3 X 3 equals.

On the seventh, I saw four Senators. . . .They had been overseas; had seen Germany, Italy, and knew all the answers. Smart men, I would say. Since Julius Caesar, such men as

Charlemagne, Richelieu, Charles V, Francis I, the great King Henry IV of France, Frederick Barbarossa to name a few, and Woodrow Wilson and Franklin D. Roosevelt have had many remedies and still could not solve the problem. Maybe these historical characters did not have the brains and background of the four "able Senators."

Anyway, their song was that France would go Communistic, so would Germany, Italy, and the Scandinavians; and there was grave doubt about England staying sane. The Pope they said, was blue as indigo about the situation. All of them except Senator —— assured me that the European world is at an end. . . . Europe has passed out so often in the last 2,000 years—and has come back, better or worse than ever, whichever pleases the fancy, that I am not impressed with cursory glances of oratorical members of the famous "Cave of the Winds" on Capitol Hill. I have been there myself and have been through crisis after crisis in each of which the country surely would disintegrate that most "Senatorial Alarm" does not much alarm me. But all four, I think, are most anxious to keep world peace.

I am making this trip, determined to work for and win the peace. I am giving nothing away except I will do anything I can to save starving and war-battered people but I hope we will be able to help people to help themselves. This is the only sound policy.

Potsdam, July 19, 1945

Stalin was a day late in arriving. It was reported that he was not feeling up to par. He called on me as soon as he arrived. It was about 11 A.M. He, Molotov, Vishinski and Pavlov stayed for lunch. We had a most pleasant conference and Stalin assured me that Russia intended to carry out the Yalta agreements and to enter the war against Japan in August. Mr. Churchill had arrived on time the day set for the conference. He had called on me as soon as he arrived in Berlin. . . .

August 5, 1945

Well, we have been away from Berlin since eight o'clock the morning of August 2nd. I am very sure no one wants to go back to that ravaged city.

Had lunch with Britain's King George VI. He is a very pleasant and surprising person. We had a short interview just before luncheon on the Renown in the King's cabin. He was very much interested in what had taken place at the Conference and in our new terrific explosion.

He showed me a sword which had been presented to Sir Francis Drake by Queen Elizabeth. It was a powerful weapon but the King said it was not properly balanced.

We had a nice and appetizing lunch—soup, fish, lamb chops, peas, potatoes and ice cream with chocolate sauce. The King, myself, Lord Halifax, a British Admiral, Admiral Leahy, Lascelles, the Secretary of State in that order around the table.

He showed me a sword
which had been presented
to Sir Francis Drake by Queen
Elizabeth. It was a powerful
weapon, but the King said it
was not properly balanced.

We had a nice and appetising
lunch soup, fish, lamb chops
peas, potatoes and ice cream
with chocolate sauce. The
King, myself, Lord Halifax, a
British Admiral, Adm. Leahy
Lascelles, the Secretary of State
in that order around the
table. Talked of most
everything, and nothing much.

Before lunch I inspected a guard of honor and complimented the British Band on the manner in which it had played the National Anthem of U. S. There was much formality, etc., in getting on and off the British Ship.

As soon as we returned to the Augusta, the King returned the call and we put on the formalities. He inspected the guard, looked over the sailors, signed the ship's guest book, collected an autograph for each of his daughters and the Queen, and after some more formalities went back for his Ship. We have been crossing the Atlantic ever since at the rate of 645 miles every 24 hours.

August 10, 1945

Up at six and ready for business. Snyder had met me at Norfolk on Tuesday evening, when we returned from Berlin, and had discussed certain bad situations developing between War Production Board and Office of Price Administration. At 9:30, got Krug in and gave him a job on reconversion, making the War Production Board the Reconversion Board and then called in Bowles and made peace between them.

At 10:15, had the scientists Bush and Conant and George L. Harrison, General Groves, Secretaries of State, War and Navy in to discuss the Atomic Bomb and how much could be published about it. A very interesting meeting. Ordered a press release for Sunday, covering its main features because some alleged scientists were spreading crazy tales about it.

Ate lunch at my desk and discussed the Japanese offer to surrender which came in a couple of hours earlier. They wanted to make a condition precedent to the surrender. Our terms were "unconditional." They wanted to keep the Emperor. We told them we would make the terms.

Had a Cabinet meeting after lunch, which was a very satisfactory one. Getting a team together. Took them into my confidence and told them all about the Japanese situation. They kept the confidence—an unprecedented thing in the immediate past.

While all this has been going on, I have been trying to get ready a radio address to the nation on the Potsdam Conference. Made the first draft on the ship coming back. Discussed it with Byrnes, Rosenman, Ben Cohen, Leahy and Charlie Ross. Rewrote it four times and then the Japanese offered to surrender, and it had to be done again. As first written it contained 4500 words and a thousand had to be taken out. It caused me a week of headaches but finally seemed to go over all right over the radio at 10 P.M. tonight.

August 11, 1945

Well, the speech seems to have made a hit according to all the papers. Shows you never can tell. I thought it was rotten.

We are all on edge waiting for the Japanese to answer.

I ███ is a pacifist 100%.
He wants us to disband our
armed forces, give Russia our
atomic secrets and trust
a bunch of adventurers in
the Kremlin Politburo who have
no morals, personal or public.
I don't understand a "dreamer"

September 20, 1945

This has been a very busy and trying week. After returning from Missouri via Paducah, Kentucky, where Senator Alben Barkley and Congressman Gregory were taken aboard the Sacred Cow, much study was given pending problems. There were several thousand people at the airport in Paducah, all of whom wanted to see Jumbo, the Cardiff Giant, the President of the United States. It is a most amazing spectacle, this worship of high office.

Barkley brought his dear old mother (87 years old) down to see me. She is a lovely old lady—just like Mamma. She thinks Alben is about the Zenith of everything just as Mamma thinks of me—and she's right as can be.

Congressman Gregory's lovely wife and beautiful daughter were at the airport to see him off. They were invited to go aboard the Cow and see how Mr. Gregory would be placed on his way to Washington. He looks like "Mr. Smith." (Smith goes to Washington.)

We arrived in the Capital City at 7:45 P.M., and Alben and I had our pictures taken as is usual when "notorious" persons leave or arrive in cities.

Went to the taxpayers' house on 16th and Pennsylvania Avenue and spent a very pleasant night in sleep.

Spent Monday morning seeing various persons. Told my staff that the whole labor set-up would be transferred to the Secretary of Labor and stated that a Justice of the Supreme Court, a Secretary of War, a Director of the Surplus Property, Disposal Authority would be announced tomorrow (Tuesday) at 4 P.M.

Created some excitement in my immediate staff.

Every morning at nine A.M. I have a conference with John Snyder, head of the Office of Reconversion, Sam Rosenman, Special Counsel, Matt Connelly, Appointment Secretary, Charlie Ross, Press Secretary, Mr. Ayers, his assistant, Bill Hassett, Secretary for correspondence, Harry H. Vaughan, Brigadier General and Military Aide, J. K. Vardaman, Commodore and Naval Aide, and Judge Latta, who looks after documents for me.

Well, when I told this group that I was transferring all labor things to Schwellenbach, the Secretary of Labor, there was consternation—but I did it.

It is almost impossible to get action around here even from the most loyal of the close helpers. It is just a natural reluctance to agree to any sort of change and a fear that something will be done to spoil the Era of Good Feeling which is now on.

I believe in this Republic, and I also believe in a strong two-party system. France went out with multiple pressure groups as did Italy and Germany.

There should be a real liberal party in this country and I don't mean a crackpot professional liberal one. The opponents to liberalism and progress should join together in the party of the opposition.

September 19, 1946

Mr. —— spent two and one half-hours talking to me yesterday. I am not sure he is as fundamentally sound intellectually as I had thought. He advised me that I should be far to the "left" when Congress was not in session and that I should move right when Congress is on hand and in session. He said F.D.R. did that and that F.D. never let his "right" hand know what his "left" hand did.

X is a pacifist 100 per cent. He wants us to disband our armed forces, give Russia our atomic secrets and trust a bunch of adventurers in the Kremlin Politbureau. I do not understand a "dreamer" like that. The German-American Bund under Fritz Kuhn was not half so dangerous. The Reds, phonies and the "parlor pinks" seem to be banded together and are becoming a national danger.

I am afraid they are a sabotage front for Uncle Joe Stalin. They can see no wrong in Russia's four and one-half million armed force, in Russia's loot of Poland, Austria, Hungary, Rumania, Manchuria. They can see no wrong in Russia's living off the occupied countries to support the military occupation.

But when we help our friends in China who fought on our side it is terrible. When Russia loots the industrial plant of those same friends it is all right. When Russia occupies Persia for oil that is heavenly although Persia was Russia's ally in the terrible German War. We sent all our supplies which went to Russia by the Southern Route through Persia —sent them with Persia's help.

The President in a memorandum on Dec. 11, 1946, expressed himself bluntly on John L. Lewis.

Lewis called a coal strike in the spring of 1946. For no good reason. He called it after agreeing to carry on negotiations without calling it. At least, he told John Steelman to tell me there would be no strike. He called one on the old gag that the miners do not work when they have no contract.

After prolonged negotiation, I decided to exercise the powers under the second war powers act and take over the mines. After they were taken over, a contract was negotiated between the Secretary of the Interior, Mr. Krug, and John L. Lewis.

The contract was signed in my office on the 5th of May, and Mr. Lewis stated for the movies that it was his best contract and would not be broken during the time of Government control of the mines.

Along in September and October, 1946, there arose some minor disputes between the Solid Fuels Administrator and Mr. Lewis. Nothing of vital importance—purely details of interpretation of the contract with regard to coal weights on which the new welfare fund is based and some other small details that could have been settled easily by a half-hour discussion.

But Mr. Lewis wanted to be sure that the President would be in the most embarrassing position possible for the Congressional elections on November 6. So he served a notice on the first day of November, that he would consider his contract at an end on a certain date. Which was in effect calling a strike on that date. He called his strike by a subterfuge in order to avoid prosecutions under the Smith-Connelly Act. But he will be prosecuted nevertheless.

The strike took place as planned by Mr. Lewis. It lasted seventeen days and then Mr. Lewis decided for the first time in his life that he had "overreached himself." He is a demagogue in action. . . .

I discussed the situation with the secretaries in the White House at the morning meeting after the strike call, and informed them that it was a fight to the finish. At the Cabinet meeting on Friday, before the election, the Attorney General was instructed to take such legal steps as would protect the Government. Discussions were held with the Cabinet and special meetings were called at which the Solid Fuels Administrator, Mr. Krug, the Secretary of Labor, Mr. Schwellenbach, the Attorney General, Mr. Clark, the Special Counselor to the President, Mr. Clifford, and the Special Assistant to the President, Dr. John Steelman were present.

The instructions were a fight to the finish. . . .

Mr. Lewis was hauled into Federal Court, fined no mean sum for contempt. Action was started to enforce the contract and I had prepared an address to the country to be delivered on Sunday evening, December 8.

Mr. Lewis folded up on Saturday afternoon, December 7, at three P.M. . . . He cannot face the music when the tune is not to his liking. . . .

He tried to get into communication with me while I was taking a sun treatment at Key West for a cold. He tried to talk to Dr. Steelman, he tried to approach the Secretary of the Navy, Mr. Forrestal, he tried to get in touch with the Secretary of Labor on the night before the fold up. For the first time, he found no pipeline to the White House. . . .

January 1, 1947

Spent New Year's Eve on the Yacht Williamsburg with the White House staff and ex-staff—eighteen of them. Gave each of them a gold seal White House card wishing a very happy New Year, signed. We had a very happy evening together.

Went to bed at 1:30 after the ship's Chief Pharmacist's Mate gave me a good pounding with alcohol. Had breakfast with my Naval Aide, Rear Admiral Foskett, and Captain Freeman, the Commander of the yacht. Came back to the White House at 8:45 A.M. New

Year's Day. Read the morning papers as usual. Some gave me hell and some did not. It makes no difference what the papers say if you are right.

Called the "boss" (Mrs. T.) at 10 A.M. and had a talk with her and the daughter. Never was so lonesome in my life. . . .

Telephoned to Byrnes, Snyder, Clark, Patterson, Forrestal, Krug, Harriman, Schwellenbach, Anderson and left word for Hannegan who was out on a fishing trip.

Then I called General Fleming, General Eisenhower, former Secretary of War Stimson, and Miss Perkins. Apparently, they were all pleased by the calls—and so was I.

Called Senator Vandenberg. Had a very pleasant conversation with him. He expressed the opinion, in answer to a question on the subject, that it would be better for me to see the Republican leaders after my State of the Union Message, on Monday, January 6, 1947, rather than before the delivery of the message.

Called Joe Martin. He assured me that cooperation was at the top of his consideration. . . .

Talked to Secretary Byrnes in White House study at 12:45 on the subject of the President of the World Bank. McCloy, former Assistant Secretary of War, is being considered but he is hesitant about taking the post. . . .

We discussed the Roosevelt agreement with Churchill and MacKenzie King on the Atomic Energy program. No one seems to have thought the thing would work out as it has. . . .

Secretary Snyder came in at 2:15. Stayed until 3:30 P.M. discussing McCloy, Byrnes, Morgenthau, labor legislation, message, etc., etc.

The President addressed The Gridiron Club on May 11, 1947. Gridiron speeches are never reported. But the President preserved his speech in a memorandum.

Glad to be here—it was a great show. You have given me a lot of hints which I know will be helpful to me.

I would like to reciprocate by discussing with you the various techniques of those citizens who are anxious to sacrifice themselves upon the altar of public service and become host to the Nation at 1600 Pennsylvania Avenue.

The last time I was here I explained to a speaker one method which had been successfully pursued. I hope that explanation proved useful.

Since then I have been observing the various methods pursued by other citizens, who seem to have other ideas on the subject—which I am sure would have a large sale among Governors and Senators.

For instance one of them is to get elected Governor of New York. That method has succeeded in the past. It may yet be a good formula. It has not always succeeded but you

THE WHITE HOUSE
WASHINGTON

I Read Tribune inquiry W.G.N.

r Read health certificate

You see my physical condition is excellent now look at that blood pressure

But blood pressures vary I've an idea that there were pressures of 290 over 180 when my car came within fourteen feet of backing into a gravel pile down in Brazil—

THE WHITE HOUSE
WASHINGTON

the result so I can run the United States and the World as it should be. I have several able men in reserve besides the present holder of the job, because I think in a week or two the present Secretary for Columnists will need the services of a psychiatrist and will in all probability end up in St. Elizabeth's! I've appointed a Secretary for Semantics — a most

---

THE WHITE HOUSE
WASHINGTON

important post He is to furnish me 40 and 50 dollar words. Tell me how to say yes and no in the same sentence without a contradiction He's tell me the combination of words that will put me against inflation in San Francisco and for it in New York. He's to show me how to keep silent — and say every thing. You can very well see how he can save me

---

Then I've appointed a Secretary of Reaction. I want him to abolish flying machines and tell me how to restore

---

THE WHITE HOUSE
WASHINGTON

oxcarts, oar boats and sailing ships What a load he can take off my mind if he'll put the atom back together so it can't be broken up. What a worry that will abolish for both me & Vishinski.

remember that old copy book admonition, "If at first you do not succeed, try, try again." Platform and policies need not be any trouble—just adopt the Democratic Platform and say you can do it better.

Perhaps a nonpolitical trip around the country far far in advance of the Convention might improve the chances of the aspirant.

Then there is a Senatorial approach. You might say that I used that myself. Get yourself elected from Ohio. One of the States known as the Mother of Presidents. . . .

There is a third way being pursued in the Senate—there are dozens of methods being pursued in the Senate. Be very shy and aloof, say you want to go home and write your memoirs. Say you would not touch the crown with a ten foot pole—refuse it at least thrice —but say nothing about just taking it in hand and wearing it at the proper time. This method may bring home the bacon.

There is another and an intriguing method known as the foreign travel method. When following this method heads of foreign states should be interviewed—particularly Uncle Joe, the Generalissimo's views should be carefully publicized. The stay-at-homes should be impressed by Stalin's love for them and it should be strongly emphasized how well Uncle Joe can talk—I repeat—talk cooperation. Who can say—it used to be from the Log Cabin to the White House. Now it may be from the Kremlin to the White House—you never can tell, it might work. We will wait and see. . . .

But seriously, Gentlemen, I want to say that whichever of these methods succeeds— and as I have said, most of them are being tested out today—this country of ours will move right along. Our system is fundamentally sound. This is the greatest governmental system in the world. Our press has helped to make it so. As I have said before, our press has done a particularly fine job in making clear to the people the full meaning of our policy of aid to Greece and Turkey. Our press can take some share of the credit for the resounding majority which the Greek and Turkish aid bill has just won in the House of Representatives.

I am not here just to butter up the press. I do not think it is perfect. But, it is the best press in the world and it is doing a fine job. It is an integral part of our democracy.

This year there was issued a memorial stamp honoring the memory of a great publisher —an immigrant, incidentally. One of his sayings is printed on that stamp. I am glad it is there so it will be read by everyone in our country. It expresses a profound truth: "Our Republic and its press will rise or fall together."

December 25, 1947

We had a most happy and pleasant Christmas, with all the brothers and Bess present. Frank, George and Fred with their wives Natalie, May and Christine with two children of Fred—David and Marian.

My sister Mary Jane came on the 22nd and I am sure spent an enjoyable time. My brother could not come—in fact, I didn't ask him because he had told me he intended to have all his family at the time. He has four boys, all married but one, and a lovely daughter. I called him and he said twenty-two sat down to dinner at his house. I am sure they had a grand dinner—a much happier one than a formal, butler-served one, although ours was nice enough. But family dinner cooked by the family mother, daughters, grand-daughters "served" by them is not equaled by the White House, Delmonicos, etc.

Shown newspaper clippings alleging that his health was bad, the President amused him-self by writing the following memorandum, using a red pencil to underscore the captions at the top and noting that he ought to read one newspaper's version of his health while having his own health certificate in front of him. This was written just before Christmas, 1947.

Columnist

Digest of views and how to run the world

Inflation

    1. Read Tribune inquiry W.G.N.

    2. Read health certificate.

You see my physical condition is excellent now. Look at that blood pressure. But blood pressures vary. I have an idea that there were pressures of 290 over 180 when my car came within fourteen feet of backing into a gravel pile down in Brazil.

You know I walk and swim and worry very little. I appoint people to responsible positions to worry for me. You have no idea how satisfactory that policy is.

I have just made some additions to my Kitchen Cabinet, which I will pass on to my successor in case the Cow should fall when she goes over the moon.

I appointed a Secretary for Inflation. I have given him the worry of convincing the people that no matter how high the prices go, nor how low wages become, there just is not any danger to things temporal or eternal. I am of the opinion that he will take a real load off my mind—if Congress does not.

Then I have appointed a Secretary of Reaction. I want him to abolish flying machines and tell me how to restore oxcarts, oar boats and sailing ships. What a load he can take off my mind if he will put the atom back together so it cannot be broken up. What a worry that will abolish for both me and Vishinski.

I have appointed a Secretary for Columnists. His duties are to listen to all radio commentators, read all columnists in the newspapers from ivory tower to lowest gossip, coordinate them and give me the result so I can run the United States and the World as it should be. I have several able men in reserve besides the present holder of the job, because I think in a week or two the present Secretary for Columnists will need the services of a psychiatrist and will in all probability end up in St. Elizabeth's.

I have appointed a Secretary of Semantics—a most important post. He is to furnish me 40 to 50 dollar words. Tell me how to say yes and no in the same sentence without a contradiction. He is to tell me the combination of words that will put me against inflation in San Francisco and for it in New York. He is to show me how to keep silent—and say everything. You can very well see how he can save me an immense amount of worry.

It is a great addition to the Kitchen Cabinet and I am sure would be of great use to my successor if the Tribune should by unforeseen chance get its wish.

But you know at this holiday season of peace on earth and good will toward men, I am going to wish everyone all happiness by hoping that my health chart remains above normal, and that no one will have a worry about becoming President, and that he gets everything he hopes for for Christmas.

I wish for everyone and all the world, peace on earth, good will toward men.

January 6, 1948

Congress meets—too bad, too.

They will do nothing but wrangle. I am to address them soon. They won't like the address either.

February 2, 1948

I am sending the Congress a Civil Rights message. They, no doubt, will receive it as coldly as they did the State of the Union Message. But it needs to be said.

February 8, 1948

I go for a walk and go to church. The preacher always treats me as a church member and not as the head of a circus. That is the reason I go to the First Baptist Church.

One time I went to the —— because I knew Reverend ——. He made a real show of the occasion. I will never go back. I do not go to church for show. I dislike headline hunters. It is too bad I am not a showman.

February 14, 1948

Saint Valentine's Day. Fog, rain and 49 degrees. My "Baby" and her best friend give me Valentines as does Bess and I could not get out to get them one. In times past I was the giver, now things are reversed. It is something to be the Chief of State.

March 6, 1948

Attend White House Correspondents' dinner at which Tony Vaccaro is made President.

March 17, 1948

I make a speech to the Congress on Russia.

I make a speech to the Friendly Sons of Saint Patrick, enlarging on my Congressional message and reading Henry Wallace out of the Democratic Party.

I flew to New York after the speech to Congress at 12:30. Reviewed the Saint Patrick's parade with Governor Dewey!

April 4, 1948

Took a walk at ten A.M. Went to the Mellon Gallery and succeeded in getting the watchman on duty to let me in. Looked at the Old Masters found in salt mine in Germany. Some very well-known paintings by Holbein, Franz Hals, Rubens, Rembrandt and others.

It is a pleasure to look at perfection, especially when you think of some of the lazy, nutty moderns. It is like comparing Christ with Lenin. May there be another awakening. We need an Isaiah, John the Baptist, Martin Luther—may he come soon, whoever he may be.

May 1, 1948

Attend a health meeting and speak extemporaneously. Seemed to go over big. This comes of the Gridiron and Editors appearance. Suppose I am in for a lot of work now getting my head full of facts before each public appearance. If it must be done, I will have to do it. Comes of poor ability to read a speech and put feeling into it.

May 6, 1948

I appeared before a family life conference at 12:30 and spoke over all four networks without a manuscript. The audience gave me a most cordial reception. I hope the radio and television audience were half as well pleased.

I may have to become an "orator." I heard a definition of an orator once—"He is an honest man who can communicate his views and make others believe he is right." Wish I could do that.

Because I think I have been right in the approach to all questions 90 percent of the time since I took over. . . .

May 7, 1948

Responses from the radio on the family life speech are very satisfactory. Looks as if I am stuck for "off the cuff" radio speeches. It means a lot of new work.

Had an important conference with Marshall, Forrestal, Snyder, Jim Webb of Budget and Forrestal's budget man. We are faced with a defense problem. I have wanted a uni-

Bess and I are eating supper on the south porch of the White House at 7 P.M. I am facing the Jefferson Memorial across the White House lawn. There is a fountain in the center of the lawn surrounded by petunias — we had dwarf cannas last year and the Jap beetles ate them into rags and tatters.

A ball game or two goes on in the park south of the lawn. Evidently a lot of competition from the cheers and calls of the coaches.

A robin hops around looking for worms; finds one and pulls with all his might to unearth him.

A mocking bird imitates, robins, jays, red birds, crows, hawks — but has no in-dividual note of his own. A lot of people like that.

Planes take off and land at the National Air Port south of the Jefferson Memorial.

It is a lovely evening!

I can see the old Chesapeake & Potomac Canal going across the Washington Monument grounds — barges anchoring west of the Mon-ument. I can see old J. Tu. Adams going versal training program, a balanced regular setup. Ground, air, water and a reserve to back up the regular skeleton training force.

The Congress cannot seem to bring itself to do the right thing—because of votes. . . . I want a balanced sensible defense for which the country can pay. . . .

Marshall is a tower of strength and common sense.

June 28, 1948

Bess and I are eating supper on the south porch of the White House at seven P.M. I am facing the Jefferson Memorial across the White House lawn. There is a fountain in the center of the lawn surrounded by petunias—we had dwarf cannas last year and the Japanese beetles ate them into rags and tatters. A ball game or two goes on in the park south of the lawn. Evidently a bit of competition from the cheers and the calls of the coaches.

A robin hops around looking for worms, finds one and pulls with all his might to unearth him.

A mocking bird imitates robins, jays, redbirds, crows, hawks—but has no individual note of his own. A lot of people like that. Planes take off and land at the National Airport south of the Jefferson Memorial.

It is a lovely evening.

I can see the old Chesapeake and Potomac Canal going across the Washington Monument grounds—barges anchoring west of the Monument. I can see old J. Q. Adams going swimming in it and getting his clothes stolen by an angry woman who wanted a job. The old guy did not have my guards or it would not have happened. Then I wake up, go upstairs and go to work.

July 14, 1948

Take the train for Philadelphia at seven P.M. eastern daylight time. Arrive in the rain at 9:15. Television sets at both ends of trip. No privacy sure enough now.

Hear Alabama and Mississippi walk out of convention. Hear Governor Donnelly nominate me. Both on the train radio. Hard to hear. My daughter and my staff try to keep me from listening. Think maybe I will be upset. I won't be.

Arrive at Convention Hall; see a horde of politicians, masculine and feminine. Have a pleasant time visiting with Barkley out on a balcony of the hall back of the stage. It was an interesting and instructive evening. I made my acceptance speech at two A.M.

July 15, 1948

Arrived in Washington at the White House at 5:30 A.M., my usual getting-up time. But I go to bed at 6:00 and listen to the news. Sleep until 9:15, order breakfast and

WITH GENERAL GEORGE C. MARSHALL

WITH GENERAL DWIGHT D. EISENHOWER

go to the office at 10:00. I called a special session of Congress. My, how the opposition screams. I am going to attempt to make them meet their platform promises before the election. That is acording to the "kept" press and the opposition leadership "cheap politics." I wonder what "expensive politics" will be like. We will see.

July 16, 1948

Editorial columns and cartoons are gasping and wondering. None of the smart folks thought I would call the Congress. I called them for July 26, turnip day at home. . . .

I am going to make a common sense, intellectually honest campaign. It will be a novelty and it will win.

July 19, 1948

Have quite a day. See some politicos. A meeting with General Marshall and Jim Forrestal on Berlin and the Russian situation. Marshall states the facts and the condition with which we are faced. I made the decision ten days ago to *stay in Berlin*. Jim wants to hedge. . . . I insist we will stay in Berlin—come what may.

Royall, Draper and Jim Forrestal come in later. I have to listen to a rehash of what I know already and reiterate my "Stay in Berlin" decision. I do not pass the buck, nor do I alibi out of any decision I make.

Went to Pershing's funeral in the marble amphitheatre. An impressive ceremony. This is the fifth time I have prepared to attend the General's funeral. It came off this time.

Bess and Margaret went to Missouri at 7:30 EDT 6:30 God's time. I sure hated to see them go. Came back and read the papers, some history and then wrote this. It is hot and humid and lonely. . . .

July 22, 1948

I go to the yacht Williamsburg to get some rest. Get some sunshine and a good night's sleep. Have a new masseur, he is good and I sleep well. I hope that Congress will do something in the public interest. I fear nothing will be done.

August 3, 1948

Took off at 8:00 A.M. Central Standard time. Arrived in Washington at 1:20 EDT just three hours and twenty minutes flying time. Think of that. Takes 27 hours by train and two days and a half by automobile. My old plane the Sacred Cow took 4½ hours. We have not adjusted ourselves to this speed.

Went to the White House. Had lunch—a short nap and went to the executive office and worked until 6:30. Found the White House "falling down." My daughter's sitting room floor had broken down into the family dining room. How very lucky we are that the thing did not break when Margie and Annette Wright were playing two piano duets where the floor broke.

The White House architect and engineer have moved me into the southeast or Lincoln Room—for safety—imagine that!

August 4, 1948

Had quite a session with secretaries Ross, Steelman, Connelly, Clifford, Hassett, Murphy, Dawson, Hopkins, Landry, Vaughan. Dennison absent. Discussed many things.

Had Barkley, Rayburn, Lucas and McCormack come in at ten. Talk over the Congressional situation. Tried to get some fighting spirit into them. Some success, I believe.

Set a press conference for tomorrow. It ought to be good.

September 10, 1948

I decide to go down the Potomac in the Williamsburg after Margie decided to go to New York.

Take her to the train at noon and return to the White House where I work, receive callers (customers, I call them) until 1:15. Get aboard the Williamsburg at 1:30 and have lunch. Take a nap and send for the sailor boy who gives me a rubdown. Charlie Ross, Clark Clifford, Connelly, the three aides, General Harry Vaughan, Captain Robert Dennison, Colonel Robert Landry, Dr. Steelman, David Noyes and Albert Carr all came aboard. We go down the Potomac to Quantico and stay all night.

September 11, 1948

Spend most pleasant day talking about world affairs, western trip, speeches, prima donnas in government, etc.

September 13, 1948

Have a terrific day.

Forrestal, Bradley, Vandenberg (the General, not the Senator), Symington brief me on bases, bombs, Moscow, Leningrad, etc. I have a terrible feeling afterward that we are very close to war. I hope not.

Discuss situation with Marshall at lunch. Berlin is a mess. Have usual Monday Cabinet luncheon. These luncheons are great. They have kept the Cabinet a team.

March 24, 1949

Mr. Churchill is coming to dinner. He came, brought me his life of John Churchill, Duke of Marlborough.

We had a grand time at dinner. General Marshall, Barkley, V.P., Acheson, Sect. of State,

THE JEFFERSON MEMORIAL

Chief Justice Fred Vinson and Mrs. Vinson, the British Ambassador all made a contribution to the evening. (This Blair Lee House is a handicap to such events.)

Mr. Churchill gave Bess his book on painting. . . .

The former P.M. . . . told me . . . he'd be Prime Minister again. . . . He may be as right as I was last year.

We had to go out and have pictures made on the "stoop." How we need the old building across the street, known as the White House.

November 1, 1949

Had dinner by myself tonight. Worked in the Lee House office until dinner time. A butler came in very formally and said "Mr. President, dinner is served." I walk into the dining room in the Blair House. Barnett in tails and white tie pulls out my chair, pushes me up to the table. John in tails and white tie brings me a fruit cup, Barnett takes away the empty cup. John brings me a plate, Barnett brings me a tenderloin, John brings me asparagus, Barnett brings me carrots and beets. I have to eat alone and in silence in candle-lit room. I ring. Barnett takes the plate and butter plates. John comes in with a napkin and silver crumb tray—there are no crumbs but John has to brush them off the table anyway. Barnett brings me a plate with a finger bowl and doily on it. I remove the finger bowl and doily and John puts a glass saucer and a little bowl on the plate. Barnett brings me some chocolate custard. John brings me a demitasse (at home a little cup of coffee—about two good gulps) and my dinner is over. I take a hand bath in the finger bowl and go back to work. What a life!

Here are memoranda dated December 9, 1950, and January 10, 1951, respectively.

We had conference after conference on the jittery situation facing the country. Attlee, Formosa, Communist China, Chiang Kai-Shek, Japan, Germany, France, India, etc. I have worked for peace for five years and six months and it looks like World War III is near.

I hope not—but we must meet whatever comes—and we will.

*   *   *

It has been a very strenuous ten days. Left Kansas City December 26, at a few minutes after ten A.M. Arrived in Washington a short time after two P.M. Had quite a reception —State, Defense, Treasury and several other cabinet members, and prominent people to meet me. General Eisenhower came to see me on Saturday, January 6, and spent an hour talking over his duties in Europe. He called me when he left his hotel and I met him at the airport. We reviewed the honor guard together and had pictures by the dozen. I gave him the best sendoff I could.

ceremony. Didn't deserve it but
that's the case in most awards.
But not in those Congressional Medals of Honor I awarded yesterday to
the survivors of five Korean heros.
Hope I'll not have to do that again.
I'm a damned sentimentalist and
I could hardly hold my voice steady
when I gave a medal to a widow
or a father for heroism in action.
    It was similar to giving citations
to the men who were shot protecting
me at the Blair House — and I
choked up just as I did then.
What an old fool I am!

We the People

of the United States, in order to form a more perfect Union, establish Justice, insure domestic Tranquility, provide for the common defence, promote the general Welfare, and secure the Blessings of Liberty to ourselves and our Posterity, do ordain and establish this Constitution for the United States of America.

Article. 1.

Section. 1. All legislative Powers herein granted shall be vested in a Congress of the United States, which shall consist of a Senate and House of Representatives.

Section. 2. The House of Representatives shall be composed of Members chosen every second Year by the People of the several States, and the Electors in each State shall have the Qualifications requisite for Electors of the most numerous Branch of the State Legislature.

No Person shall be a Representative who shall not have attained to the Age of twenty five Years, and been seven Years a Citizen of the United States, and who shall not, when elected, be an Inhabitant of that State in which he shall be chosen.

Representatives and direct Taxes shall be apportioned among the several States which may be included within this Union, according to their respective Numbers, which shall be determined by adding to the whole Number of free Persons, including those bound to Service for a Term of Years, and excluding Indians not taxed, three fifths of all other Persons. The actual Enumeration shall be made within three Years after the first Meeting of the Congress of the United States, and within every subsequent Term of ten Years, in such Manner as they shall by Law direct. The Number of Representatives shall not exceed one for every thirty Thousand, but each State shall have at Least one Representative; and until such enumeration shall be made, the State of New Hampshire shall be entitled to chuse three, Massachusetts eight, Rhode-Island and Providence Plantations one, Connecticut five, New-York six, New Jersey four, Pennsylvania eight, Delaware one, Maryland six, Virginia ten, North Carolina five, South Carolina five, and Georgia three.

When vacancies happen in the Representation from any State, the Executive Authority thereof shall issue Writs of Election to fill such Vacancies.

The House of Representatives shall chuse their Speaker and other Officers; and shall have the sole Power of Impeachment.

Section. 3. The Senate of the United States shall be composed of two Senators from each State, chosen by the Legislature thereof, for six Years; and each Senator shall have one Vote.

Immediately after they shall be assembled in Consequence of the first Election, they shall be divided as equally as may be into three Classes. The Seats of the Senators of the first Class shall be vacated at the Expiration of the second Year, of the second Class at the Expiration of the fourth Year, and of the third Class at the Expiration of the sixth Year, so that one third may be chosen every second Year; and if Vacancies happen by Resignation, or otherwise, during the Recess of the Legislature of any State, the Executive thereof may make temporary Appointments until the next Meeting of the Legislature, which shall then fill such Vacancies.

No Person shall be a Senator who shall not have attained to the Age of thirty Years, and been nine Years a Citizen of the United States, and who shall not, when elected, be an Inhabitant of that State for which he shall be chosen.

The Vice President of the United States shall be President of the Senate, but shall have no Vote, unless they be equally divided.

The Senate shall chuse their other Officers, and also a President pro tempore, in the Absence of the Vice President, or when he shall exercise the Office of President of the United States.

The Senate shall have the sole Power to try all Impeachments. When sitting for that Purpose, they shall be on Oath or Affirmation. When the President of the United States is tried, the Chief Justice shall preside: And no Person shall be convicted without the Concurrence of two thirds of the Members present.

Judgment in Cases of Impeachment shall not extend further than to removal from Office, and disqualification to hold and enjoy any Office of honor, Trust or Profit under the United States: but the Party convicted shall nevertheless be liable and subject to Indictment, Trial, Judgment and Punishment, according to Law.

Section. 4. The Times, Places and Manner of holding Elections for Senators and Representatives, shall be prescribed in each State by the Legislature thereof; but the Congress may at any time by Law make or alter such Regulations, except as to the Places of chusing Senators.

The Congress shall assemble at least once in every Year, and such Meeting shall be on the first Monday in December, unless they shall by Law appoint a different Day.

Section. 5. Each House shall be the Judge of the Elections, Returns and Qualifications of its own Members, and a Majority of each shall constitute a Quorum to do Business; but a smaller Number may adjourn from day to day, and may be authorized to compel the Attendance of absent Members, in such Manner, and under such Penalties as each House may provide.

Each House may determine the Rules of its Proceedings, punish its Members for disorderly Behaviour, and, with the Concurrence of two thirds, expel a Member.

Each House shall keep a Journal of its Proceedings, and from time to time publish the same, excepting such Parts as may in their Judgment require Secrecy; and the Yeas and Nays of the Members of either House on any question shall, at the Desire of one fifth of those Present, be entered on the Journal.

Neither House, during the Session of Congress, shall, without the Consent of the other, adjourn for more than three days, nor to any other Place than that in which the two Houses shall be sitting.

Section. 6. The Senators and Representatives shall receive a Compensation for their Services, to be ascertained by Law, and paid out of the Treasury of the United States. They shall in all Cases, except Treason, Felony and Breach of the Peace, be privileged from Arrest during their Attendance at the Session of their respective Houses, and in going to and returning from the same; and for any Speech or Debate in either House, they shall not be questioned in any other Place.

No Senator or Representative shall, during the Time for which he was elected, be appointed to any civil Office under the Authority of the United States, which shall have been created, or the Emoluments whereof shall have been encreased during such time; and no Person holding any Office under the United States, shall be a Member of either House during his Continuance in Office.

Section. 7. All Bills for raising Revenue shall originate in the House of Representatives; but the Senate may propose or concur with Amendments as on other Bills.

Every Bill which shall have passed the House of Representatives and the Senate, shall, before it become a Law, be presented to the President of

Congress may by general Laws prescribe the Manner in which such Acts, Records and Proceedings shall be proved, and the Effect thereof.

Sect. 2. The Citizens of each State shall be entitled to all Privileges and Immunities of Citizens in the several States.

A Person charged in any State with Treason, Felony, or other Crime, who shall flee from Justice, and be found in another State, shall on Demand of the executive Authority of the State from which he fled, be delivered up, to be removed to the State having Jurisdiction of the Crime.

No Person held to Service or Labour in one State, under the Laws thereof, escaping into another, shall, in Consequence of any Law or Regulation therein, be discharged from such Service or Labour, but shall be delivered up on Claim of the Party to whom such Service or Labour may be due.

Sect. 3. New States may be admitted by the Congress into this Union; but no new State shall be formed or erected within the Jurisdiction of any other State; nor any State be formed by the Junction of two or more States, or Parts of States, without the Consent of the Legislatures of the States concerned as well as of the Congress.

The Congress shall have Power to dispose of and make all needful Rules and Regulations respecting the Territory or other Property belonging to the United States; and nothing in this Constitution shall be so construed as to Prejudice any Claims of the United States, or of any particular State.

Sect. 4. The United States shall guarantee to every State in this Union a Republican Form of Government, and shall protect each of them against Invasion; and on Application of the Legislature, or of the Executive (when the Legislature cannot be convened) against domestic Violence.

Article. V.

The Congress, whenever two thirds of both Houses shall deem it necessary, shall propose Amendments to this Constitution, or, on the Application of the Legislatures of two thirds of the several States, shall call a Convention for proposing Amendments, which, in either Case, shall be valid to all Intents and Purposes, as Part of this Constitution, when ratified by the Legislatures of three fourths of the several States, or by Conventions in three fourths thereof, as the one or the other Mode of Ratification may be proposed by the Congress; Provided that no Amendment which may be made prior to the Year One thousand eight hundred and eight shall in any Manner affect the first and fourth Clauses in the Ninth Section of the first Article; and that no State, without its Consent, shall be deprived of its equal Suffrage in the Senate.

Article. VI.

All Debts contracted and Engagements entered into, before the Adoption of this Constitution, shall be as valid against the United States under this Constitution, as under the Confederation.

This Constitution, and the Laws of the United States which shall be made in Pursuance thereof; and all Treaties made, or which shall be made, under the Authority of the United States, shall be the supreme Law of the Land; and the Judges in every State shall be bound thereby, any Thing in the Constitution or Laws of any State to the Contrary notwithstanding.

The Senators and Representatives before mentioned, and the Members of the several State Legislatures, and all executive and judicial Officers, both of the United States and of the several States, shall be bound by Oath or Affirmation, to support this Constitution; but no religious Test shall ever be required as a Qualification to any Office or public Trust under the United States.

Article. VII.

The Ratification of the Conventions of nine States, shall be sufficient for the Establishment of this Constitution between the States so ratifying the Same.

The Word "the," being interlined between the seventh and eighth Lines of the first Page, the Word "Thirty" being partly written on an Erazure in the fifteenth Line of the first Page. The Word "is" being interlined between the thirty second and thirty third Lines of the first Page and the Word "the" being interlined between the forty third and forty fourth Lines of the second Page.

Attest William Jackson Secretary

done

done in Convention by the Unanimous Consent of the States present the Seventeenth Day of September in the Year of our Lord one thousand seven hundred and Eighty seven and of the Independance of the United States of America the Twelfth In witness whereof We have hereunto subscribed our Names,

G⁰. Washington—Presidt and deputy from Virginia

Delaware
Geo: Read
Gunning Bedford jun
John Dickinson
Richard Bassett
Jaco: Broom

Maryland
James McHenry
Dan of St Thos. Jenifer
Danl Carroll

Virginia
John Blair—
James Madison Jr.

North Carolina
Wm. Blount
Richd. Dobbs Spaight.
Hu Williamson

South Carolina
J. Rutledge
Charles Cotesworth Pinckney
Charles Pinckney
Pierce Butler.

Georgia
William Few
Abr Baldwin

New Hampshire
John Langdon
Nicholas Gilman

Massachusetts
Nathaniel Gorham
Rufus King

Connecticut
Wm. Saml. Johnson
Roger Sherman

New York
Alexander Hamilton

New Jersey
Wil: Livingston
David Brearley
Wm. Paterson
Jona: Dayton

Pennsylvania
B Franklin
Thomas Mifflin
Robt. Morris
Geo. Clymer
Thos. FitzSimons
Jared Ingersoll
James Wilson
Gouv Morris

Bess, Margie, and Mrs. Wallace came in at 7:30 A.M. Saturday, January 6. Bess went to New York, yesterday, January 9th, to go to a show with Margie. Friday night, January 5th, I went to the Gaiety to see Edward Arnold in the "Apple of his Eye."

Monday, the 8th, I went to Congress and gave them all I could in the message on the State of the Union. Apparently, it was all right. Telegrams and letters are running 15 to 1 favorably. Never worked so hard on a speech. All say it showed effort. Hope it does some good.

Received the Woodrow Wilson Award today. A wonderful medal with a great citation on the back. Mrs. McAdoo, Mr. Sayre, and other highest of the high hats present. It was quite a ceremony. Did not deserve it but that is the case in most awards. But not in those Congressional Medals of Honor I awarded yesterday to the survivors of five Korean heroes. Hope I will not have to do that again. I am a damned sentimentalist and I could hardly hold my voice steady when I gave a medal to a widow or a father for heroism in action. It was similar to giving citations to the men who were shot protecting me at the Blair House—and I choked up just as I did then. What an old fool I am!

III

Here are undated memoranda dealing with various questions.

The Congress has passed a resolution for a Constitutional Amendment, limiting the terms of the President to two. That resolution should have also contained a provision for two terms for Senators—twelve years, and for members of the House—twelve years. It should have contained a provision that House members should have a period of service of four years. That is, the House of Representatives should be elected with the President for a four-year term of service. Then the country would be able to vote into or out of power a President, a legislative majority and one-third of the Senate at every general election.

The twelve-year limitation for members of the House and Senate would prevent the fossilization of the Key Committees. At present some of the Committees of the House and Senate have men who live in a day before yesterday or back before the First World War. There are some who, if they think at all, think of the time when Champ Clark was Speaker of the House and "Five-cent Cigar" Tom Marshall was Vice President. There are others who look a little beyond Tom Marshall and Champ Clark—they even turn to Thomas B. Reed in their backward thinking. There are old-time Senators who even make Louis XIV of France and George III of England look like shining Liberals.

A two-term, twelve-year service would remedy this.

Twelve years of Washington is enough for any man. After twelve years of service, no President, Senator or member of the House of Representatives should be eligible for re-election.

We would help to cure senility and seniority—both terrible legislative diseases nationally —if twelve years were the limit of service for President, Senator and Congressman.

There is a growing tendency on the part of the Senate to infringe on the powers and prerogatives of the President. . . . The Congress has a right to investigate and pass laws to remedy those things which are not done correctly by the Executive. But the Congress has no right to interfere or hamper the President in the enforcement of the laws passed by the Congress.

In Andrew Johnson's administration Congress tried to override the Constitution in this respect and finally impeached the President when he would not perform the unconstitutional acts Congress passed.

Grover Cleveland was harassed the same way although he was not impeached. The 80th Congress made every effort possible to abolish the powers of the President and were turned out of office for it.

When men are tried and abused publicly by irresponsible Senators who hide behind their immunity it is almost hopeless to try to get good men for responsible positions.

This memorandum, written by the President, is an introduction to the "State of the Union Speech" to the Eighty-first Congress which the President could not deliver because of shortage of radio time, but the President said he expressed the sentiments contained in it to many Senators and Representatives in person and considered it a worthy addition to his private papers.

Members of the 81st Congress—Written but not delivered.

1st Kings III:9

Give therefore thy servant an understanding heart to judge thy people, that I may discern between good and bad; for who is able to judge this thy so great a people?

II Chronicles I:10

Give me now wisdom and knowledge, that I may go out and come in before this people: for who can judge this thy people, that is so great?

On my first appearance before the Congress after I became President I quoted to you the prayer of King Solomon, quoted it and expressed to you a hope for divine guidance and for help and cooperation from this august body and from the people of the United

States. Until the wars ended on September 2, 1945, I received that help and cooperation. But when my peace-time policy message came to this body on September 6, 1945, a campaign of vilification, misrepresentation and falsehood was inaugurated against me. It was successful in that it brought about the election of a bitter opposition Congress—with the final results you are well acquainted.

Now I have no bitterness in my heart against anyone—not even the bitter opposition press and its henchmen the paid columnists and managing editors and the bought and paid for radio commentators. Never in the history of the country did a President need the honest help and cooperation of Congress, press and people as I needed them in September, 1945.

It seems to have been necessary for the President to go through three and one-half years of travail.

Now here we are with a new start, a majority vote of all the people saying that they believe in me.

Now all I want to do is to carry out that people's mandate. I only want peace in the world and a fair deal for every part of the population of this great nation. I want your help and cooperation. The majority of this great body was elected on the platform with me. You have learned that the people do not believe in the kept press and the paid radio and that they have no patience with the man who lets a poll be his conscience.

We have the greatest republic in the world if we remember that the people elect us to do what we think is right and not what some pollster or misguided editorial writer tells us to do. I pray God constantly for guidance. I hope you will do that too. Then this great country which God has chosen to lead the world to peace and prosperity will succeed in that undertaking.

Now for the message on the State of the Union.

IV

Here are some notes from the President's daily appointments list.

Oct. 19, 1945—Major General Patrick J. Hurley, American Ambassador to China.
        Lieutenant General Albert C. Wedemeyer
        Discussed China. I told them my policy is to support Chiang Kai-Shek.

November 15, 1945—Attached longhand note
        Chinese set up. We should make it plain that we are mopping up the war with

Japan. That there are more than 1,000,000 Japanese soldiers in central China. That Russia, Britain and United States have recognized the Central Government under Chiang Kai-Shek. That Stalin says the Chinese Communists are not. We are merely winding up the war.

November 27, 1945—Longhand memo attached

Phone Mrs. Roosevelt to be one of our five delegates to Assembly of the United Nations Organization.

She said Yes. November 27, 1945.

February 18, 1947—The Secretary of State (Marshall)

The more I see and talk to him, the more certain I am he's the great one of the age. I am surely lucky to have his friendship and support.

October 30, 1947—Longhand memo attached—to discuss—the Secretary of State.

1. When to present the Marshall Plan to Congress
    (a) How to implement an administrative setup.
    (b) Where should the Administrator be located?
2. The military implications of a satellite attack
    (a) Do we need a plan to meet this.
    (b) Should we proceed to make one.

PART FOUR

Forebears and Biographical Notes

I

PRESIDENT TRUMAN is a descendant of early American pioneers who came from England, Northern Ireland and Germany. These pioneers settled in New England, New York, Maryland and Virginia and some of their many offspring moved westward to Kentucky and Ohio and thence to Missouri and others farther south to South Carolina and Texas.

Most of his forebears based their lives on the land, either as landed gentry or farmers, and many took active part in local community life as officials of one sort or another, and as soldiers.

The land still has a strong hold on President Truman who, "like Cincinnatus," hopes to return to the "plow" in the remaining years of his life. The President still owns the farm that Solomon Young, his maternal grandfather, settled on near Grandview, Missouri, in 1842.

The four grandparents of the President were born in Kentucky. On his father's side, Anderson Shippe Truman lived near Bagdad in Shelby County and Mary Jane Holmes about three miles northwest of Shelbyville. On his mother's side, Solomon Young lived south of Long Run station and Harriet Louise Gregg had her home three miles northwest of Simpsonville. All of his grandparents migrated to Missouri about one hundred years ago. They were among the earliest settlers of Westport Landing, which today is Kansas City, Missouri.

President Truman was born in Lamar, Missouri. The birth certificate shows only "Harry S. Truman." I asked the President what the "S" stood for. The President explained, "I was supposed to be named Harrison Shippe (Shippe is spelled both with and without an 'e' in the family records) Truman, taking the middle name from my paternal grand-father. But others in the family wanted my middle name to be Solomon, taken from my

[151]

ANDERSON SHIPPE TRUMAN   MARY JANE HOLMES TRUMAN

maternal grandfather. But apparently no agreement could be reached and my name was recorded and stands simply as Harry S. Truman."

President Truman, as he pointed out earlier in this book, is a collateral descendant of President Tyler. In addition to the Tyler name, one finds in the Truman family tree names chronicled in colonial and early American history, such as Doniphan, Shippe, Duvall, Ijams and Cheney.

The President is not interested in a family tree as such, but more in the type of life people lead than in their ancestry. With a twinkle in his eye he repeats the often quoted line of Mark Twain that if you search a family tree far enough you may eventually find the gibbet. But he proudly adds that as far back as he has had time or interest to go, one fact stands out: "There has never been any scandal in the family."

The President continued, "Miss Ethel Noland, a cousin of mine, is the only authority on the ancient connections of my family. But the interesting thing is that in going through the story of all the aunts and great-aunts and great-uncles there has never been any disgrace in the family of any kind—and no divorces. Isn't that something!

"I don't like divorces because I think that when you make a contract, you should keep it. The marriage contract is one of the most sacred in the world.

"No contract should be entered into lightly. I don't give my word lightly. When I say I'm going to do something, I do it, or bust my insides trying to do it.

"But I have never followed all those genealogical details of my family.

"The Trumans came from England. And my mother's family, that is her mother's grandparents, came from Ireland—Northern Ireland. My grandfather Young's great-grandfather came from Germany. So that is a pretty good mixture.

"The first Truman is supposed to have come to this country in 1666, but I don't know whether he was an ancestor of mine. I'm told that his father was the one who built the big brewery in England in 1665. There are a lot of Trumans in Maryland, some in New York, some in Ohio and some in South Carolina."

II

In a nostalgic mood one evening in his book-crowded study in Blair House, President Truman talked about his father and mother.

The President said, "My father was a very energetic person. He worked from daylight to dark, all the time. And his code was honesty and integrity. His word was good. When he told us that something was a fact with regard to a horse or a cow or a sheep or a piece of land, that was just what it was. It was the truth. And he raised my brother and myself to put honor above profit. He was quite a man, my dad was. He was not a talker. He was a doer. He lived what he believed, and taught the rest of us to do the same thing.

"My mother was the same sort of person. She taught us the moral code and started us in Sunday school. She was always interested in our school programs, and our place was always the gathering place for all the kids in the neighborhood because my mother liked children and liked to see them have a good time, and liked to help them have a good time.

"She taught us the right thing and made us do it.

HARRIET L. YOUNG   SOLOMON YOUNG

"When the minister went out to see mamma when she was sick the last time—I guess it was the time before the last, when she had the broken shoulder—and he said, 'You ought to be mighty proud of your son in Washington,' mamma said, 'I am, but I've got another son I am just as proud of, and I have a daughter that I am just as proud of.'

"One of the funniest things she said when I brought her to Washington in the plane and got her off at the airport and all the photographers and newsmen crowded around her was, 'Oh, fiddlesticks, why didn't you tell me about this and I would have stayed at home.' "

I asked the President whether his mother ever inspired any special thoughts in him about the Presidency. He said:

"My mother tried to make me a good boy and a good man. She had no political ambitions for me."

III

When I saw the President three days later, he handed me a twelve-page longhand script. The President said he had sat up into the early morning hours after I had left him that evening at Blair House when he was reminiscing about his father and mother.

He said very simply that he had written something down about his early life.

The President said, "Here are some notes that may be of interest."

With his permission I am printing them just as I got them. In the days that followed, whenever I would see him of a morning, he would quietly hand me further notes. They follow, divided in parts as he gave them to me.

THE FIRST PART

My first memory is that of chasing a frog around the back yard in Cass County, Missouri. Grandmother Young watched the performance and thought it very funny that a two-year-old could slap his knees and laugh so loudly at a jumping frog.

Then I remember another incident at the same farm when my mother dropped me from an upstairs window into the arms of my Uncle Harrison Young, who had come to see the new baby, my brother Vivian.

We moved from the Cass Co. farm to the old home of my mother's father in Jackson County. Grandfather Truman lived with us and he made a favorite out of me, as did my Grandfather Young.

I can remember when my Truman grandfather died. All three of his daughters were present, Aunt Ella, Aunt Emma and Aunt Matt. I was four years old and was very curious about what was happening. Grandpa Truman was a grand man and petted me a great deal. He was a strong Baptist.

I was also a great favorite of Grandpa Young's. He'd take me to the Belton Fair with him and I'd sit in the Judges' Stand and watch the races—Grandpa was a judge.

My brother Vivian was two years my junior and he had lovely long curls. Grandpa and I cut off his curls one day by putting him in a highchair out on the south porch. Mamma was angry enough to spank us both, but she had such respect for her father that she only frowned at him. One day after the hair cutting episode I sat on the edge of a chair in front of the mirror to comb my hair—I fell off the chair backwards and broke my collar-

THE BIRTHPLACE OF HARRY S. TRUMAN AT LAMAR, MO.

My first memory is that of
chasing a frog around the
backyard in Cass County, Mo.
Grandmother Young watched
the performance and thought
it very funny that a two year
old could slap his knees and
laugh so loudly at a jumping frog.
Then I remember another
incident at the same farm
when my mother dropped me
from an upstairs window into
the arms of my Uncle Harrison
Young, who had come to see
the new baby, my brother Vivian.

MRS. JOSEPH TILFORD NOLAN
AUNT OF PRESIDENT TRUMAN

MARTHA ELLEN YOUNG TRUMAN
MOTHER OF HARRY S. TRUMAN

bone—my first but not my last broken bone. Later in this same room I was eating a peach and swallowed the seed. Almost choked to death but mamma pushed the seed down my throat with her finger and I lived to tell about it.

Vivian and I used to play in the south pasture—a beautiful meadow in bluegrass. At the end of the grove was a mudhole. This grove was row on row of beautiful maple trees, a quarter of a mile long and six rows wide. We had a little red wagon which we took with us on our adventures in the pasture. We finally wound up at the mudhole with a neighbor boy about our age and I loaded Vivian and John Chancellor into the little wagon, hauled them into the mudhole—and *upset* the wagon. What a spanking I received. I can feel it yet! Every stitch of clothes on all three of us had to be changed, scrubbed and dried, and so did we!

My father bought me a Shetland pony about this time, and a beautiful little saddle— my brother's granddaughter has the saddle now. I'd ride with my father on my little Shetland and he on his big horse. He'd lead my pony and I felt perfectly safe—but one day coming down the north road toward the house I fell off the pony and had to walk about half a mile to the house. My father said that a boy who was not able to stay on a pony at a walk ought to walk himself. Mamma thought I was badly mistreated but I wasn't, in spite of my crying all the way to the house. I had learned a lesson.

When I was five and Vivian was three we were presented with a sister—Mary Jane, named for her grandmother Truman. We heard her cry upstairs and thought we had a new pet until father told us we had a new sister.

When I was six, Vivian three, and Mary one year old, we moved to Independence. Mamma was anxious we should have town schooling. About this time my eyes became a problem and mamma took me to Dr. Thompson in Kansas City. Dr. Thompson was the brother-in-law of Dr. Charlie Lester, the son of the family physician in Civil War times, and himself the family doctor by succession. Glasses were fitted by Dr. Thompson and I've worn practically the same prescription ever since. When I first put the glasses on I saw things and saw print I'd never seen before. I learned to read when I was five but never could see the fine print. I've been "fine printed" many a time since I've been able to read it.

When I was eight I started to school at the Noland School on South Liberty Street. My First Grade teacher was Miss Myra Ewing, a grand woman. That first year in school made a profound impression on me. I learned to get along with my classmates and also learned a lot from Appleton's *First Reader*, learned how to add and subtract, and stood in well with my teacher.

In my second school year Miss Minnie Ward was my teacher and she was a good teacher and a lovely woman.

Along in January my brother and I had terrible cases of diphtheria—no antitoxin in those days. They gave us ipecac and whiskey. I've hated the smell of both ever since.

The family sent Mary Jane to the farm so she wouldn't catch the disease. Old Letch, the husband of our cook and washwoman, Caroline Simpson, took Mary Jane to the farm in a big farm wagon, driving a fine team of horses. It took nearly all day to make the trip, and her safe arrival was not known for two more days until old Letch returned.

Aunt Caroline (Aunty we called her) and her husband Letch worked for us from the time we moved to Independence. There were five children in Aunty's family—an older girl named Amy whom I never saw, Sam, Horace, Claude and Delsie. Sam (Fat Sam) afterwards became the fireman at the County Home and stayed there until he died. Horace went insane, as did his father, Letch. Claude became an efficient Pullman porter and died on the job. Delsie is still alive, a cripple from her teens.

My brother and I recovered from our illness and I went to summer school to catch up to the Third Grade. A new schoolhouse had been built in the meantime—the Columbian. Next door to the school lived a lovely old lady who had helped nurse me to health after

JOHN ANDERSON TRUMAN AND HIS BRIDE
MARTHA ELLEN YOUNG
PARENTS OF HARRY S. TRUMAN

HARRY AND VIVIAN TRUMAN
AGED SIX AND FOUR

my terrible experience with diphtheria. I was paralyzed for six months after the throat disease left me, and my mother wheeled me around in a baby buggy. My arms, legs and throat were of no use, but I recovered and went back to school and skipped the. Third Grade. Then I went to the Fifth with Aunt Nannie Wallace as the teacher. She was a wonder of a teacher—had been at it for thirty years and knew her job.

When we first moved to Independence my mother took us to Sunday school at the Presbyterian Church. I was six years old. In my Sunday school class was a beautiful little girl with golden curls. I was smitten at once and still am—she's Mrs. Truman and the mother of the loveliest daughter *"in the world."*

After the Seventh Grade course at the Columbian School we all went to high school at the old Ott School on North Liberty St. We had wonderful teachers, Prof. Palmer, Miss Hardin (afterwards Mrs. Palmer), Miss Tillie Brown, Miss Sallie Brown, Miss Maggie Phelps, Miss McDonald and Prof. Patrick, Prof. Bryant and Prof. Baldwin, Supt. of Schools. All of them made a contribution to the knowledge and character of the students. It was a great class. Besides the present First Lady, there were in it Charles G. Ross, a great journalist and Press Secretary to the President, a great physician and surgeon, Dr. Elmer Twyman, son and grandson of great doctors. His father was our doctor in the diphtheria cases, along with Dr. Charlie Lester. I slammed the cellar door on my foot and cut off the end of my big toe on the left foot. Mamma held it in place until Dr. Tom Twyman, Elmer's father, put some iodoform on it and it stayed put and got well!

Miss Phelps held special classes for a neighbor boy and myself preparing us for West Point or Annapolis. These studies were in the evening. The other boy made it to Annapolis. I failed because of poor eyesight.

THE SECOND PART

In 1896 we moved to a nice house at Waldo Ave. and River Blvd. Before we left the house on Chrysler Street, I remember my father's discovery of gas in the back lot where he was drilling a water well. Water was struck at 140 feet but it was sulphur water and the stock wouldn't drink it. So a deeper well was drilled in the same hole. Two strata of gas and one of oil were hit. We had the old house piped for gas, put in a gas tank, and for a while we had an ideal setup. Then the oil choked off the gas and my father traded for the Waldo Ave. property. There was a cupola or tower on the northwest corner of the Chrsyler St. house and when Cleveland was elected in 1892, the rooster weathervane on top of the tower was properly decorated and my father rode a gray horse in the torchlight victory parade.

There were a lot of new boys and girls in the Waldo Ave. neighborhood. We had many a grand time with them. In the Spanish-American War we organized a .22 rifle company, elected a captain and marched and countermarched, camped out in the woods just a block or two north of our house, and had a grand time. Not one of the boys was over fourteen.

On White Oak Street, a block south, lived two Houchens boys, sons of a preacher. At the east end of White Oak at Union St. lived two Chiles boys—Henry and Morton. Across Waldo at Woodland College was Paul Bryant. Two doors east on Waldo was Jim Wright, and next door east on Waldo were five girls and three boys—the Burrus'.

Down on Delaware, two blocks east of River Blvd., lived the Paxtons and the Wallaces, with the Sawyers on the corner of Waldo and Delaware St. The grand times we

HARRY S. TRUMAN
AT THE AGE OF THIRTEEN

had! Halloween parties and all sorts of meetings after school, making bridges by Caesar's plans and discussing what we'd like to be when grown up. We published a high school paper in 1901, called *The Gleam* for Tennyson's "Follow the Gleam." It is still published by the Independence High School after fifty years.

It was a grand class. Most of them made good. One of them became President of the United States, and one the First Lady. Nearly all the others lived happily and were good citizens.

My father and I made a trip to Oregon County to see about a piece of land he owned. It was a great trip. We crossed a little river by fords, thirteen times in eight miles, found the forty acres running up the side of an Ozark mountain. It wasn't worth a nickel.

I'd obtained a job with a railroad contractor named L. J. Smith. He paid me $35.00 a month to keep time for four hundred hobos. Every two weeks I had to pay them off —in a saloon in Independence or in Sheffield. The hobos would spend all their earnings in the saloon and be back at work on Monday. They received $1.50 a day for ten hours and paid $3.50 a week for board, so about $11.00 was all they could get for two weeks' work. Three dollars a day was paid for a wagon & team and driver. That is where I learned about minimum wages!

I was with the contractor six months and received about a hundred dollars after deductions. Then I went to work in the mailing room of the *Kansas City Star* at seven dollars a week. About that time in the latter part of 1902, we moved to 2108 Park Ave. in Kansas City and I went to work for the National Bank of Commerce at $35.00 a month. After a year I was receiving $60.00 and then went to the Union National at $75.00 a month— a very good salary in 1904. Joined a new National Guard organization in 1905.

I'd tried for both West Point and Annapolis under the tutelage of my history teacher, Miss Margaret Phelps, and failed physically on account of my short sight.

NANCY TYLER HOLMES
GREAT GRANDMOTHER OF
PRESIDENT TRUMAN

This was a beautiful
blue uniform with
red trimmings.
I was twenty one then.
H.S.T.

But the Guard wasn't so particular so I was accepted as a private. Went to Camp Girardeau in August, 1905 and acted as No. 1 on the old 3-inch light piece. Went to camp year after year for six years. We moved to the old home farm in 1906 and I became a real farmer. Plowed, sowed, reaped, milked cows, fed hogs, doctored horses, baled hay and did everything there was to do on a six-hundred-acre farm with my father and my brother. But we never did catch up with our debts. We always owed the bank something—sometimes more, sometimes less—but we always owed the bank.

My father died in 1914. My brother had married and was running a farm of his own. In 1917, I rejoined and helped organize a National Guard regiment and became a 1st Lieutenant in it. Went to Camp Doniphan at Ft. Sill, Okla. Went to school, ran a canteen and drilled with Battery F. Was examined for promotion in February, 1918, sent overseas with an advance regimental detail in March. Left N. Y. on the night of Mar. 30, 1918 on the *George Washington*, landed in Brest, France, on April 13, 1918, was sent to the 2nd Corps Field Artillery School at Montigny-sur-Aube in charge of Dick "By God" Burleson, brother-in-law of Gov. Vardaman of Mississippi and nephew of the Postmaster General. He and Col. Robert M. Danford (afterwards Major Gen. Chief of Field Artillery) taught me how to fire a 75 battery.

Along in October, notice caught up with me that I was a captain. I'd been in command of Battery D, 129th, since July 11th.

I fired 3000 rounds of 75 ammunition from 4 a.m. to 8 a.m., Sept. 26, 1918. I had slept in the edge of a wood to the right of my battery position on Friday night. If I hadn't awaked and got up at 4 a.m. I would not be here, because the Germans fired a barrage on my sleeping place! At 8 o'clock my battery pulled out for the front. As we marched on a road under an embankment, a French 155 mm. battery fired over my head and I still have trouble hearing what goes on when there is a noise. I went back and told the French Captain what I thought of him but he couldn't understand me—so it made no difference.

We came to the front line at a little town, what was left of it, called Buirrelles. I stopped the Battery and went forward with my executive officer and the battalion commander, Major Gates. We located a battery of the enemy and sat in a ditch while they fired machine guns over us. Finally went back to the Battery and spent the rest of the night getting it across no man's land. At 5 a.m., the 28th of Sept., the operations officer of the regiment, Major Paterson, came to my sleeping place under a bush and told me to fire a barrage in ten minutes! I told him I couldn't figure one in ten minutes but I'd try!

Didn't fire a shot but moved on up behind the infantry. Finally went into position on a road between Varennes and Cheppy about 10 p.m., Sept. 28. In going into position I rode my horse under a tree and a limb of the tree scraped my glasses off—and I picked them up from the horse's back behind the saddle! No one would believe a tale like that but it happened. I put the Battery into position and then moved into an orchard a half mile ahead

FIRST LIEUTENANT HARRY S. TRUMAN

the next day. Fired on three batteries, destroyed one and put the other two out of business. The Regimental Colonel threatened me with a court martial for firing out of the 35th Division sector! But I saved some men in the 28th Division on our left.

One of my lieutenants was acting as communications officer that afternoon and had a phone set on his head. He looked up and saw a German plane and remarked to the Battery Exec. that the so & so German was dropping something. The bomb went off and cut the phone off his head and didn't hurt him. In the meantime I was up in front of the infantry without a weapon of any kind, observing the enemy fire from every direction. An infantry sergeant came up to my foxhole and told me that my support had moved back 200 yards, and that I'd do well to come back too. I did!

THE THIRD PART

One day in late 1908 a cousin of my mother's had come over to the farm to look at some stock and I noticed a Masonic pin on his coat. I told him I'd always wanted to be a member. A few days later he brought me an application for membership in Belton Lodge No. 450 at Belton, Missouri. On Feb. 9th, 1909, I received my first degree. Frank Blair was President of the Bank of Belton where we did our banking, and W. B. Garrison was cashier—or Frank was cashier and Billy was assistant cashier. Anyway both were enthusiastic Masons. Frank was Deputy Grand Master and District Lecturer for the 34th Masonic District of Missouri, and Billy Garrison was Master of Belton Lodge. These two men very patiently taught me the lectures and the ritual of the various degrees. I received my 3rd degree on March 9, 1909, and shortly after that the Grand Lecturer of Missouri, James R. McLachlan of Kehoka, came to Belton for a three-day stay. I attended every meeting for the three days and then followed the Grand Lecturer to Holden and to St. Joseph, became letter perfect in all three degrees and would accompany Frank Blair on his official visits in the 34th District. There were nine or ten lodges in the district and during the winter months all of them were visited. At the next lodge election I was elected Jr. Warden and served during 1910.

In 1911 I organized a Lodge at Grandview—No. 618—and was made Master U.D. along in May or June. Went to the Grand Lodge meeting in St. Louis and obtained a charter for Grandview and became a regular attendant at the yearly meetings of the Grand Lodge.

The 22nd Masonic District, which was Jackson County as a whole, was split into two districts and in 1924, on the death of the Deputy Grand Master for the new 59th Dist., I was appointed Deputy Grand Master and Deputy Grand Lecturer, served five years and was appointed into the Grand Lodge Line of Officers by William R. Gentry, Grand Master in 1930. At that time I was the Presiding Judge of the County Court of Jackson County and a working Democrat. Mr. Gentry is a rabid Republican! I went up the line in the usual way until I arrived at the first elective office which is the 4th one from the top. A fight was organized in St. Louis against me but I won out. That fight continued until I was elected Grand Master of Missouri in 1940. I was in the midst of the bitterest campaign of my career in that year for re-election to the Senate. I was out against the Governor for the nomination and against Manville Davis who was the Republican nominee in the general election.

Davis became very bitter in the campaign and made some awful charges against me. I had a Catholic political friend in St. Louis by the name of James E. Wade. He attended a meeting in a county north of the Missouri River and not far from St. Louis. Davis made his usual charges. Forrest Donnell who afterwards became Governor and Senator was speaking from the same platform. Donnell was just behind me in the Grand Lodge Line and would be Grand Master in a year or two.

So Jim Wade went up to him after this north Missouri meeting and asked him if I could be the low sort of fellow that Davis charged and still be Grand Master of Masons of Missouri. Mr. Donnell said, "No, Jim, he could not." That ruined Mr. Davis—I won by 276,000 votes.

I finished out my term as Grand Master, did my job as Senator and evidently came out well with both. I made more than twenty trips by air to Missouri from September, 1940, to September, 1941, to transact the business of the Grand Lodge, gave half my salary as Grand Master to the Masonic Service Association for the soldiers in camps, organized the Committee for the Investigation of the Defense Program in the Senate in Feb. 28, 1941, and succeeded in getting myself into all kinds of trouble—Vice President— President, etc.

I owe a great deal of my familiarity with the Bible to my Masonic studies—and to the fact that I read it through twice before I was twelve years old.

In April, 1917, after Mr. Wilson asked for a declaration of war, those of us who had any military experience went to work to help win the war. It became my duty to help expand my old National Guard Battery B into a regiment, and Battery C in Independence into two batteries for that regiment. Battery A in St. Louis was also trying to expand into a regiment.

We succeeded in expanding B & C into a regiment and we also raised a battery for the St. Louis regiment. I thought I'd do well to be a sergeant—but when F Battery was organized I became a first lieutenant. It almost scared me to such an extent that I was afraid I'd never make good.

Harry B. Allen, a neighbor and schoolmate of mine, was made Captain of Battery F. A former cavalry second lieutenant, West Point graduate, son-in-law of one of Kansas City's big brewers, was made Colonel of the 2nd Missouri Field Artillery—in federal service the 129th Field Artillery—35th Division. We were sworn into federal service at Kansas City on August 5, 1917. On September 26, 1917 we entrained for training at Ft. Sill, Okla., at Camp Doniphan. The Colonel made me "canteen" officer of the regiment. I asked Eddie Jacobson, a member of Battery F and a man with merchandise experience, to run the canteen for me. We collected two dollars per man from each battery, headquarters and supply company. Twenty-two hundred dollars in all. Eddie and I set up a store, a barber shop and a tailor shop. We went to Oklahoma City and stocked up our store. Each battery and company was ordered to furnish a clerk for the store. Eddie and I deposited our sales intake every day. In six months we paid each battery and company all the money paid in for capital, and fifteen thousand dollars in dividends. In addition to my duties as

GILBERT TRUMAN, NEPHEW OF THE PRESIDENT,
AND HIS WIFE PAULINE

HARRY TRUMAN, NEPHEW OF THE PRESIDENT,
WITH HIS WIFE, DOROTHY, AND DAUGHTER WANDA LEE

canteen officer I did all the duties of a battery officer. Took my turn as officer of the day, equitation officer, firing instruction officer for the Battery—went to Ft. Sill School of Fire as an observer and did foot drill and whatever else was to be done. When it came time for Captain Allen to make an efficiency report on one of his lieutenants, he made such a good one that the C.O. sent it back with the comment that "no man could be that good."

I came up for examination for promotion in February, 1918. Was picked for the Overseas School Detail, left Camp Doniphan Mar. 20, 1918, arrived in Rosedale, Kansas, now Kansas City, Kansas, by Rock Island Railroad, asked a switchman if I could call my fiancée in Independence and he said, "Call her, the phone's yours, but if she doesn't break the engagement at four o'clock in the morning she really loves you." I talked to her and she didn't scold me. She's Mrs. Truman. I also called my mother and sister. They all wept a little but all of them were, I think, glad to know an overseas lieutenant and to be related to him. People of the right sort were really patriotic in those days. They are at this date—but too often only the unpatriotic are publicly quoted.

THE FOURTH PART

On Oct. 27, 1918, we were moving along the road in France from one front line zone to another when a French newspaper was distributed along the line. Headlines in black letters informed us that an armistice was on. Just then a German 150 shell burst to the right of the road and another to the left.

One of the sergeants remarked, "Captain, those G.D. Germans haven't seen this paper." Another tough old sergeant remarked after these two explosions, "My God, I've swallowed my chew!" On Nov. 7 Roy Howard sent a message to the USA announcing a false armistice. Such false newspaper reports are terrible things.

We went into new positions on Nov. 6 and prepared barrages for the drive on Metz for Nov. 7. The 129th F.A. was supporting the 81st (Wild Cat) Div.

On Nov. 11, at 5 a.m., Major Paterson, the regimental operations officer, called me and told me that there would be a cease fire order at 11 a.m.—that was Nov. 11, 1918. I fired the Battery on orders until 10:45 when I fired my last shot on a little village—Hermaville—northeast of Verdun. The last range was 11,000 meters with the new D shell. Eighty-eight hundred meters was the extreme range of the 75 mm. gun with regular ammunition, but with the streamlined D shell it would reach 11,500 meters.

We stopped firing all along the line at eleven o'clock, Nov. 11, 1918. It was so quiet it made your head ache. We stayed at our positions all day and then crawled into our pup tents that evening.

There was a French battery of old Napoleon six-inch guns just behind my battery position. These old Napoleon guns had wheels six feet in diameter and no recoil mechanism. They'd run back up tall wooden contraptions built like a carpenter's sawhorse and then run down into place again. If a gunner got in the way either going or coming he'd lose an arm or a leg or any other part of his anatomy that happened to be in the way of the old gun. It was a good gun, though, and would hit the target if laid by an expert.

Along in the evening all the men in the French battery became intoxicated as result of a load of wine which came up on the ammunition narrow gauge. Every single one of them had to march by my bed and salute and yell, "Vive President Wilson, Vive Captain, Artillerie American." No sleep all night, the infantry fired Very pistols, sent up all the flares they could lay their hands on, fired rifles, pistols and whatever else would make noise, all night long.

Next day we had orders to leave our guns in line and fall back to the echelon. After that we spent our evenings playing poker and wishing we were at home.

On Dec. 7 a number of officers were given a leave. I was one of them. We went to Paris where we spent three happy days. I heard "Manon" at the Grand Opera, went to the Opera Comique to hear "Carmen," and to the Folies Bergère, a disgusting performance. Then we went to Nice, stayed at the Hotel Mediterranée, went to the American Bar in the Hotel Negresco and the one in the Rhule et Anglee. We then went to Monaco and visited the Casino at Monte Carlo, but we couldn't play because we were in uniform.

They gave us a 5-franc chip and that's all we had from the famous gambling hell.

We had lunch one day in the Casino de Paris. There were about seven or eight of us sitting at a big round table in the rear of the place, when all of a sudden every waiter in the place rushed to the front and began bowing and scraping, and we were informed that Madame la Princesse de Monaco had come in. Our Lt. Col. was facing the front and could see the performance. He watched very closely and pretty soon he reported, "Oh, hell, she's taking beer! Can you imagine a princess drinking beer?" It gave all of us common people a letdown.

We went back to the regiment, moved a couple of times, and finally landed back in Brest where we took off for U.S.A. on April 9th, 1919, landing in N. Y. on Sunday—Easter Sunday morning, April 20th. I'd been gone from that city just a year and twenty days. I made a resolution that if old lady Liberty in N. Y. harbor wanted to see me again she'd have to turn around.

We were sent to Camp Mills and then ordered to Camp Funston, at Fort Riley, Kansas, for discharge. The discharge was accomplished on May 6, 1919.

I'd been a soldier—an artilleryman—for almost two years, been under fire, lost my business connections and so I went home to the farm.

Eddie Jacobson, as fine a man as ever walked, had been my canteen manager at Camp Doniphan, Ft. Sill, Okla. It was the most successful one there. Eddie's good management and honesty caused me to be promoted and become a member of the 35th Division Overseas Detail.

When I arrived at home, Eddie and I decided to open a furnishing goods store. He'd been in that business when the war came and I knew his merchandising ability. I furnished the money and he furnished the experience. We leased a store on West 12th St. opposite the Muehlebach Hotel and bought $35,000 worth of merchandise and did a thriving business for two years. We sold over $70,000.00 worth of merchandise in a year and a half and showed a very good profit after all expenses.

We had a chance to sell out at inventory price about this time but neither of us wanted to sell. So we bought more goods and then old man Mellon's wringing out process came along—and did he wring Ed and me out!

Our inventory was worth $40,000.00 one week and the next it was worth $5,000.00. We went broke. Our creditors drove Eddie into bankruptcy, but I became a public official and they couldn't do that to me. Eddie and I continued to pay and settle our obligations, and after about fifteen years cleaned them all up honorably. Not one of our creditors, merchandisers or banks ever accused us of a dishonorable act. A couple of bankruptcy lawyers caused us a lot of trouble, but they didn't get anywhere.

In July or August, 1921, a meeting of the leaders in eastern Jackson County was held and it was decided that I should be a candidate for Judge of the County Court for the

Eastern District. County courts in Missouri consist of three judges. Two are district judges and one is elected at large for the whole county. It is an administrative body. Taxes are levied by the Court, and expenditures for roads, homes for aged, schools for delinquent children, and the insane in state institutions are supported by orders of the Court on the County Treasurer. The only really judicial act the Court performs is to make a finding of insanity when such finding is recommended by two reputable physicians.

In that county campaign in 1922 there were five candidates for Eastern Judge, a banker in Blue Springs, a fine man, supported by the Shannon faction (called rabbits) whose name was Montgomery, a real estate man named James Compton, a road contractor named George Shaw, a busted merchant named Harry Truman, supported by Pendergast (the goats), and a man named Parent from Oak Grove, a road overseer.

It was a hot campaign. Every township and precinct was visited by me. I had kinfolks all over the county, and the people I was not related to Mrs. Truman was. I won in the primary for a wonder by a plurality of 500 votes! Then my troubles began. The election was a walkaway. All the Democrats on the ticket won in the county. There were three Democrats on the County Court and they promptly managed a vicious political fight among themselves. The Presiding Judge was a Shannon man and the two District Judges were "goats." We promptly took all the jobs, but we ran the county on an economy basis which was a real one.

But in 1924 the rabbits bolted the ticket and the two District Judges were beaten. My only child was born that year and I was broke and out of a job. But I had a lot of friends and pulled through until 1926 when I was elected Presiding Judge of the County Court of Jackson County by a majority of 16,000 votes. That was the beginning of a fantastic political career that ended in the White House. It does not seem possible that it could happen. It could not happen anywhere but in the United States.

When I took over as the executive officer of the County I found its road system a wreck, its court houses falling down, its finances in such condition that the state was threatening to send the five or six hundred insane it was caring for back to the County and leave them on the court house steps. There were $2,000,000.00 or more of protested warrants out, bearing 6% interest. I went to work. I employed a county counselor, the best lawyer in the County, a purchasing agent (I fired him later when I found him in partnership with people who sold things to the County), and two or three other administrators in key jobs, and set up a system of audits and inspections which gave the crooked contractors an awful pain. I inspected every institution in the County every week and fired people right and left who didn't work in the public interest. I offered a bond issue to the taxpayers for roads and public buildings, succeeded in getting the Republican highway engineer to cooperate with me and appointed a bipartisan board of engineers, spent ten million dollars for one of the finest road systems in the country, built two new court houses and a County

HOUSE ON THE FARM OWNED BY PRESIDENT TRUMAN.
IT ADJOINS THE FARM OF HIS BROTHER VIVIAN AT GRANDVIEW, MO.

FRED TRUMAN, NEPHEW OF THE PRESIDENT,
AND HIS WIFE AUDREY

THE COURTHOUSE AT INDEPENDENCE, MO.

hospital, refinanced the County's floating debt, reduced the interest rate on County borrowing from 6% to 2½% and put the whole County setup in good shape. When I came up for re-election in 1930 my majority was 55,000.

In 1934 the County job was finished. I was maneuvered into running for the Senate in primary, just as I had been in the primary in the County in 1922.

Two fine men were my opponents. Congressman Jacob L. (Tuck) Milligan of Richmond, Mo., Senator Clark's candidate, and Jack Cochran, the *St. Louis Post-Dispatch* candidate from St. Louis. I went into sixty counties, made from six to sixteen appearances every day, and won by a plurality of 44,000. The election was a walkaway and I went to Washington.

I became a member of the Appropriations, Interstate Commerce, Public Buildings and

Grounds, Enrolled Bills, and Audit and Control committees. I attended every meeting of every committee to which I was appointed. I became vice-chairman of the Interstate Commerce Committee's subcommittee to investigate the railroad finance situation, was Chairman of the Interstate Commerce subcommittee that wrote the Civil Aeronautics Act, was on a half dozen subcommittees of the Appropriations Committee and worked closely with Sen. Tom Connally who was Chairman of the Public Buildings and Grounds Committee. That committee introduced a bill for the purpose of finishing the Capitol Building. The central section of the building has never been finished. It is a shame. The "new" dome is seven feet over the central porch and the building on which it rests is of red sandstone.

When the House and Senate wings were added and the dome was placed over the sandstone center section, it was intended by the architect of 1863 that the center stairway on the east side of the Capitol building should be moved out in proportion to the House and Senate stairways, and that the red sandstone of the old original building should be covered with the same marble as the two wings are built of. The dome also should be covered by the same sort of marble.

A little pinheaded Congressman from Iowa interested the *Washington Star,* and the House beat the bill. We still have a red sandstone center to the Capitol of the greatest republic in the history of the world, and one of the three great domes of the world hanging in the air! What an accomplishment for a pinheaded Congressman and a newspaper!

That same "great" newspaper tried the same tactics when I was making the south front of the White House architecturally correct—but, the "great" paper didn't have a pinheaded congressman to legislate—and it failed in its wrong purpose.

THE FIFTH PART

In 1934 my tour of duty as Presiding Judge of the County Court of Jackson County was drawing to a close. To sum up: I'd given the County a road system, straightened out its finances, built two new court houses and a hospital for the aged and so I thought my job was done.

In redistricting the state in 1932 for Congressional districts I had set up the 4th District with eastern Jackson County and two or three eastern city wards in Kansas City. I hoped to represent that district in the Congress of the United States. I could have stayed there the rest of my life. The organization had other ideas. I was forced into the Senate race after having told all my friends and relatives I wouldn't run for the Senate.

But ran for the nomination and won it. The election was a pushover on a New Deal platform and so I went to the Senate! My colleague, the Hon. Bennett Champ Clark was very courteous to me, escorted me to the ceremony when I was sworn in, introduced me to

SCENE DURING REMODELING OF WHITE HOUSE, 1951

the Senators and the Vice President, showed me the barber shop and the bath house and was as kind as could be.

My committee experience was an education. On the Interstate Commerce Committee I learned the history of railroad finance, civil aeronautics, communications, federal trade and became acquainted with several able and and distinguished Senators.

Same experience on Appropriations. Learned how budgets are made and unmade and learned a lot about government finance, railroad finance, air transportations' troubles, public buildings and grounds and Senatorial investigations.

I asked Senator Wheeler, Chairman of the Interstate Commerce Committee, if it would be all right for me to attend the hearings on the investigation of railroad finance. He, of course, said it would. I became the vice-chairman of that subcommittee because I was the only Senator who was always present. There were many things that came before that sub-committee. I learned a lot about finance and about federal courts. I made a report to the Senate and finally wound up as co-author of the Wheeler-Truman Bill of 1940.

In February of 1941 I introduced a resolution to establish the Committee for the Investigation of the Defense Program. Hon. James F. Byrnes of South Carolina was chairman of the Audit and Control Committee, which had to pass on my resolution. There was some delay. I had asked for $25,000 to start off my proposed committee. Eventually the liberal Sen. Byrnes agreed to the resolution with an authorized appropriation of fifteen thousand dollars!

After the resolution and the appropriation had passed the Senate, I called the Attorney General, Mr. Jackson, and asked him to recommend a counselor to me. He did, and a good one—Mr. Hugh Fulton.

I gave Mr. Fulton more than half my appropriation as salary and went to work. After our first report we were able to obtain all the funds we needed.

I began to study the operations of the famous Civil War Commission on the Conduct of the War. Vandenberg, Brewster, Taft and one or two other influential Senators tried to get me to make a Committee on the Conduct of the War out of my Committee. Thank goodness, I knew my history and I wouldn't do it.

I went to see the President and told him what I wanted to do. Explained to him that I wanted to help him win the war, that I would keep him informed of what I found and that if he could remedy the situation, he'd hear no more from me beyond that. I also went to see General Marshall and told him the same thing.

I finally had nine Senators on the Committee with me and there was never a minority report! The President, the Chief of Staff of the Army and the Chief of Naval Operations, all came to believe that the Committee was trying to help and not to hurt anyone. How I wish that today as President I had cooperation such as I gave. When fifty reporters voted

MISS MARY JANE TRUMAN
SISTER OF THE PRESIDENT

MR. AND MRS. VIVIAN TRUMAN

on the ten men who had made the greatest contribution to the war effort, I was the only legislator in the list!—which did not help my standing in the Senate.

When the National Democratic Convention was to meet in Chicago in 1944 I was a delegate and was elected to be Chairman of the Missouri delegation. As I was about to leave Independence on Friday before the Convention was to meet, Hon. James F. Byrnes called and asked me if I would nominate him for Vice President, as the President wanted him to have that position on the ticket. I said surely I'll do it if the President wants it done. Before I could get to the automobile and start for Chicago with my wife and daughter, Senator Barkley called and asked me to nominate him for Vice President. I reported my conversation with Senator Byrnes and told Barkley I was committed.

Bess, Margie and I got in the car and I drove to Chicago. When we arrived I found that I was the Missouri member of the Resolutions Committee, which committee writes the platform. I worked diligently on the platform and went to see all the leaders I knew, labor and others, to try to get them for Byrnes for Vice President. Each time I saw a leader he would tell me he was for Henry Wallace first and for me second. I told all of them that I was not a candidate. I reported all these interviews to Mr. Byrnes. He would tell me each time that Roosevelt would publicly say he was for him for Vice President.

On Wednesday, after President Roosevelt had been nominated, Bob Hannegan, the Chairman of the Democratic National Committee, came to see me at the Stevens Hotel and told me that the President wanted me to be the nominee for Vice President on the ticket with him. I was flabbergasted. I told Hannegan that I wanted to stay in the Senate, and that I would not take the nomination.

On Thursday afternoon before the V.P. nomination was to take place, I was asked to come over to the Blackstone Hotel for a conference. Of course, I went. There I found all the Democratic leaders of the nation and they began to put pressure on me, the country boy, to stand for the nomination for Vice President. Finally Mr. Hannegan called President Roosevelt in San Diego, California. Roosevelt asked Mr. Hannegan if he had received a commitment from the Junior Senator from Missouri. Mr. Hannegan told the President that he had never been in contact with as mulish and contrary a man. Then the President said, and I could hear him, "Well if he wants to let the Democratic party and the country down in the midst of a war that is his responsibility."

I was, to put it mildly, stunned.

I stood around for at least five minutes and then I said, "I'll do what the President wants."

But I had a family situation to meet. Mrs. Truman and Margie would not be happy. I knew that very well. But both were good soldiers when I told them what had happened.

After the nomination and my return to the hotel with police and Secret Service none of us were happy. But we all faced the situation and have been facing it ever since.

THE NATIONAL ARCHIVES

IV

On the morning of January 15, 1952, at 9:30, before holding his daily staff meeting in the executive offices of the White House, the President gave me a sheaf of hand-written notes and said:

"These are some notes concerning my relations with the Pendergast organization. They should belong with those I have already given you."

They were dated January 10, 1952, and follow:

There has been much speculation about my relationship politically with T. J. Pendergast (Tom). He became a powerful political boss in Missouri after 1926. His career ended in the early 1940's.

I joined a new National Guard Battery of Light Field Artillery on June 14, 1905. It was Battery B, 1st Battalion Missouri Field Artillery.

When World War 1 came on April 6, 1917—that was the date the United States declared war on the Central Powers—Battery B in Kansas City and Battery C in Independence were expanded into a regiment of six batteries and headquarters and supply companies.

MISS MARY JANE TRUMAN WITH BOYHOOD
HISTORY BOOKS OF THE PRESIDENT

This regiment became the 129th F. A. 35th Division. It was trained at Camp Doniphan, Ft. Sill, Okla.

In Battery B at Camp Doniphan was a young man by the name of James M. Pendergast, son of Michael J. Pendergast, older brother of T. J. Pendergast.

I became very well acquainted with young Jim during the war and when I came back I married and established my residence at Independence.

In 1922, it became necessary to elect an eastern judge for the county court, an administrative body similar to county commissioners in other states.

Along in July or August 1921 Jim Pendergast brought his father M. J. to see me at the little store Eddie Jacobson and I were operating on West 12th Street in Kansas City.

Mike Pendergast was head of the "goat" organization in the old 10th Ward of Kansas City and was recognized in the country part of Jackson County as the head of the Pendergast organization outside Kansas City. M. J. asked me if I would consider the nomination to the County Court from the Eastern District. I told him I would. I had been road overseer in Washington Township where the family farm is located and Postmaster of Grandview before World War 1 came along.

Well, to make it short, I filed for Eastern Judge at the proper time in 1922. There were four other candidates. A banker at Blue Springs, by name Emmett Montgomery, a fine man, was endorsed by the "rabbits," another Democratic faction in the City and County, headed by Joseph B. Shannon, afterward Congressman from the Fifth Mo. District for a long time. A road building contractor by the name of George Shaw was another candidate. He had no factional backing. Tom Parent, a road overseer at Oak Grove, had the backing of Miles Bulger, presiding judge of the county court, and a number of road overseers. James Compton, an Independence real estate man, was the fifth candidate.

I made a house to house canvass, went to every political meeting and won the nomination. Even the "goat" organization didn't think I could do it. When it came time for re-election in 1924 the "rabbits" bolted the ticket because of differences over patronage and I was defeated by a nice old Republican harnessmaker in Independence, who afterwards became locally famous for that feat.

I went to work after my defeat but kept up my political contacts. In 1926 the factions patched up their differences. In the spring, Kansas City adopted a new city manager style charter and the Democrats elected five of the nine councilmen and appointed Henry McElroy city manager. He had been my colleague on the county court from the Western District which was Kansas City.

I was nominated and elected Presiding Judge of the County Court in the fall election and took office Jan. 1, 1927.

Then I had my first contacts with T. J. Pendergast and Joseph B. Shannon. They were interested in county patronage and also in county purchases. The court appointed the purchasing agent, county welfare officers, a county auditor, heads of homes, approved the budgets of elected officials of the county, such as treasurer, county clerk, circuit clerk, county collector, county assessor, county highway engineer.

The court made up of three men is an administrative and not a judicial setup. Also appointed road overseers and various other officials. There were about nine hundred patronage jobs and they could be the foundation of a political organization. T. J. Pendergast was interested in having as many friends in key positions as possible but he always took the position that if a man didn't do the job he was supposed to do, fire him and get someone who would. I always followed such a policy.

Hixon's, Lawrence, Kansas

MARTHA ANN TRUMAN
NIECE OF THE PRESIDENT

HOME OF THE TRUMANS
ON CHRYSLER STREET
1890 TO 1896
REMODELED

HOME OF THE TRUMANS
AT 909 W. WALDO AVENUE
1896 TO 1902
REMODELED

In 1928 the "city" decided to ask for an election to authorize a bond issue for traffic ways, an auditorium, a city hall, a sewer system and several other things including a water plant and the purchase of a bridge across the Missouri River.

I decided to ask for a county bond issue at the same time for a road system, two new court houses, and a county hospital. Pendergast told me that a county bond issue would not carry. I told him that if I told the voters how I would handle it that it would carry.

I went to the people and told them that I would appoint a bipartisan board of engineers to oversee the road construction and that I would employ the two best known firms of architects in town to handle the building program, with a consulting architect from out of the state.

The county bond issue carried by a three fourths majority instead of the required two thirds. I appointed the engineers and the local architects. Then I took my private car—not a county one—and drove to Shreveport, Denver, Houston, Racine, Milwaukee, Buffalo, Brooklyn, Lincoln, Baton Rouge and several other places and looked at the new public buildings, met the architects and contractors, inspected the buildings and finally decided to employ the architect of the court house at Shreveport as consulting architect for our county buildings.

When the Court was ready to let the first road contracts Mr. Pendergast called me and told me that he was in trouble with the local road contractors and would I meet and talk with them. I told him I would. I met them with T. J. P. present. They gave me the old song and dance about being local citizens and taxpayers and that they should have an inside track to the construction contracts. I told them that the contracts would be let to the lowest bidders wherever they came from and that the specifications would be adhered to strictly. T. J. turned to his friends and said "I told you that he's the contrariest man in the county. Get out of here." When they were gone he said to me "You carry out your commitments to the voters." I did just that. But this was a three man court and the two bosses, Pendergast and Shannon, had the power to interfere with me but they didn't use it. Tom Pendergast was always a man of his word with me. My handling of the county business became a credit to the Democratic organization.

After eight years as Presiding Judge I left the county with a road system equal to any in the country, refinanced its floating debt and a set of public buildings that the people could be proud of.

I was elected to the Senate in 1934 over severe opposition in the primary.

Two distinguished Congressmen ran against me. Hon. John Cochran of St. Louis, the Post Dispatch candidate and the Hon. Jacob L. Milligan of Richmond, Mo. the Kansas City Star and Bennett Clark candidate.

By going into sixty of Missouri's 114 counties I won the nomination by a plurality of over 40,000 votes and was easily victorious in the general election on a support Roosevelt platform—which I did when I arrived in Washington.

VIVIAN TRUMAN, BROTHER OF THE PRESIDENT,
WITH HIS SONS, JOHN C., FRED, HARRY AND GILBERT

T. J. Pendergast never talked to me about my actions as county judge—except in the routine matter of party patronage and that one time when he supported me on the bond issue contracts. He only got in touch with me once when I was in the Senate and that was when Senator Alben Barkley was running for floor leader. Jim Farley called Mr. Pendergast and asked him to call me and "tell" me to support Barkley. Pendergast called me from Colorado Springs and I told him that I was pledged to Pat Harrison of Mississippi because Pat had asked me to vote for him and that Pat had made some speeches for me in the Missouri campaign, and that I'd stand by Senator Harrison. T. J. said "I told Jim that if you were committed you'd stand by your commitment, because you are a contrary Missourian." I voted for Pat and told Barkley in advance that I would. When Barkley was elected I supported him loyally.

On no other occasion did T. J. Pendergast ever talk to me about my actions in the Senate. In his prime he was a clear thinker and understood political situations and how to handle them. His word was better than the contracts of most businessmen. His physical breakdown in 1936 got him into serious trouble.

I never deserted him when he needed friends. Many for whom he'd done much more than he ever did for me ran out on him when the going was rough. I didn't do that—and I am President of the United States in my own right!

Because Pendergast was convicted of income tax fraud and went to federal prison at Leavenworth, he has been used by people opposed to me in an effort to discredit me. But nobody has ever been able to hurt me politically by slander and abuses. Nobody ever can.

Because every man has to stand on his own record and his own code of honesty and morality.

Politics force men into contacts with all manner of people but men of principle need never surrender them in order to gain or to hold political office.

For example, after I was through in the county at home, several grand juries, both state and federal, went over my career as a county judge with a fine tooth comb and of course they could only give me a clean bill of health.

V

Long before Mr. Truman came to Washington, he started to keep written records of his thoughts and the events through which he was living. They make fascinating reading and should become available when time will sanction publication.

In 1934, on the eve of making his first bid for the United States Senate, Mr. Truman wrote a long memorandum, portions of which are released for this book.

Here it is on the stationery of the Pickwick Hotel, Kansas City, Missouri, dated May 14, 1934:

Tomorrow, today rather, it is 4 A.M., I am to make the most momentous announcement of my life. I have come to the place where all men strive to be at my age, and I thought two weeks ago that retirement on a virtual pension in some minor county office was all that was in store for me.

When I was a very young boy, nine or ten years old, my mother gave me four large books called Heroes of History. The volumes were classified as "Soldiers and Sailors," "Statesmen and Sages" and two others which I forget now. I spent most of my time reading those books, Abbott's Lives and my mother's big Bible. When I was twelve I had read the Bible all the way through twice besides all the extra reading matter in the back of it. I remember that there were a number of stories about Biblical heroes with what I thought were beautiful illustrations. They impressed me immensely. I also spent a lot of time on the 20th Chapter of Exodus and the 5th, 6th and Seventh Chapters of Matthew's Gospel. I am still, at fifty, of the opinion that there are no other laws to live by, in spite of the professors of psychology.

In reading the lives of great men, I found that the first victory they won was over themselves and their carnal urges. Self-discipline with all of them came first. I found that most of the really great ones never thought they were great, some of them did. I admired Cincinnatus, Hannibal, Cyrus the Great, Gustavus Adolphus of Sweden, Washington and Lee, Stonewall Jackson and J. E. B. Stuart. Of all the military heroes Hannibal and Lee were to my mind the best because while they won every battle they lost the war, due to crazy politicians in both instances, but they were still the Great Captains of History. I found a lot of heroes were made by being in at the death or defeat of one of the really great. Scipio, Wellington, and U. S. Grant are the most outstanding. I was not very fond of Alexander, Attila, Genghis Khan, or Napoleon because while they were great leaders of men they fought for conquest and personal glory. The others fought for what they thought was right and for their countries. They were patriots and unselfish. I could never admire a man whose only interest is himself.

When I was about six or seven years old my mother took me to Sunday School and I saw there the prettiest sweetest little girl I'd ever seen. I was too backward even to look at her very much and I didn't speak to her for five years.

From the fifth grade in school until my graduation from High School we were in the same classes. If I succeeded in carrying her books to school or back home for her I had a big day.

When High School was finished my father's finances became entangled and I went to work, first as a timekeeper on a railroad; second as a single wrapper for the Kansas City Star, and then a bank clerk in the National Bank of Commerce, Kansas City. It took all I received to help pay family expenses and keep my brother and sister in school.

Then when I was twenty-two we arranged to move back to my mother's old home farm of some six hundred acres. It belonged to my mother's mother, a wonderful old woman. She had red hair and was of Scotch-Irish parentage from Kentucky. She would tell us stories of her pioneering days in Jackson County in the 1840's when we urged her. She was a very quiet, determined woman and the grandchildren all thought she was right in everything and I think she was. She raised her family while her husband took ox team freight trains to Salt Lake City and San Francisco, ran the farm and did whatever was to be done without complaint. She lived to be ninety-one and every member of her family and her neighbors sincerely regretted it when she died.

My father, brother and myself ran the farm for ten years and I had the best time I ever had in my life. We raised corn, wheat, oats, potatoes, hogs and fed some cattle. I set up and operated all sorts of farm machinery and really liked to do it. Then the world war came. I had always been a Democrat naturally because my father and mother had lived here on the border between Kansas and Missouri. Their older relatives were in the Confederate Army and they became Rebel Democrats. When I was twenty-one I joined the National Guard. Battery B was organized on Flag Day 1905 and I joined. When I showed my beautiful blue full dress uniform to my old red haired grandmother she gave me the only scolding she ever did and told me not to bring it in the house again. I had to be diplomatic with that uniform.

Soon after we moved back to the farm I began going to call on my school girl sweetheart. I'd never had another and never have. When the world war came we were ready to get married but since I had to go I didn't think it was right to get married and maybe come home a cripple and have the most beautiful and sweetest girl in the world tied down. So we waited until I came home.

The world war made a tremendous impression on me. I'd studied history to some extent and was very much interested in politics both at home and in Europe. When Germany invaded Belgium my sympathies were all on the side of France and England. I rather felt we owed France something for Lafayette. When we got into the struggle I helped organize the 2nd Mo. Field Artillery. Old B Battery was expanded into a regiment. I was elected a first lieutenant in Battery F although I only expected to be a sergeant or maybe a second lieutenant. It was quite a blow to my mother and sister for me to leave the farm.

My father had died in 1915—a sad blow to me because we were real partners. He thought I was about right and I know he was. I was with him the night he passed on and I have never forgotten it. My brother had married and was the father of twins. He'd moved to an adjoining farm and that left me in complete charge of both my uncle's and my mother's farms. My old grandmother had left all her property to my mother and her old bachelor brother for whom I was named. It was quite a responsibility but I tried to make a go of it. So when the war came along I left my sister in charge with a hired man and pulled out for Camp Doniphan.

* * *

When I was ordered up for promotion, old Gen. Lucien G. Berry conducted the examination and his object was not to find how much we knew, but how much we did not know. When we could answer, it displeased him but when we couldn't he'd rattle his false teeth, pull his handlebar mustache and stalk down the room yelling at us. "Ah, you don't know, do you? I thought you were just ignorant rookies. Now you aspire to be officers and gentlemen sure enough by becoming captains in the United States Army. It will be a disaster to the country to let you command men, etc., etc." But the old devil finally passed us all and some two or three months later commissions as captains followed us all over France. The examination was in February, the commissions were dated in April and I got mine in October.

My mother and sister came to see me at Camp Doniphan. My mother was sixty-five years old but she never shed a tear, smiled at me all the time and told me to do my best for the country. But she cried all the way home and when I came back from France she gained ten or fifteen pounds in weight. That's the real horror of war.

*   *   *

July 11, 1918, at 6:30 A.M. I took command of the Battery and I was the most thoroughly scared individual in that camp. Never on the front or anywhere else have I been so nervous. But I took over and kept command of the men until the end of the war. They'd march, fight, shoot or do anything for me and when we parted company on May 6, 1919, they gave me a silver cup a foot high all engraved with things I didn't deserve.

When we were discharged I went home. On June 28, 1919, I was married to my boyhood sweetheart.

*   *   *

Along about in 1915 I met a promoter by the name of Jerry Culbertson, through one of our farmer neighbors. This neighbor, a good man by the name of Tom Hughes, had been sheriff of Cass County at the same time that Jerry had been prosecuting attorney of the same county. Mr. Hughes had invested in several gold mines with Mr. Culbertson, none of which had made any returns on the investment.

Mr. Culbertson interested Mr. Hughes and me in a zinc lead mine at Commerce, Okla., and I undertook to run it, along with a red haired hoisting engineer by the name of Bill Throop. Bill was all wool and a yard wide but we couldn't make our mine pay. He asked me to raise $2500.00 and buy a drilling machine and go up north of Picher, Okla., and prospect the land up there for lead and zinc. But I'd already put all my ready money into the Commerce mine and couldn't raise the $2500.00. If I'd done it we'd be rolling in wealth today. The Commerce mine petered out and I lost $2,000.00. Mr. Culbertson then organized an oil company and Hughes and I were suckers enough to go into it. Some $200,000.00 was raised and leases were bought in Texas, Okla. and Kansas. At the time the war came we had a well down nine hundred feet on a 320 acre lease at Eureka, Kansas. I got all patriotic and joined the army. My partners got into a fuss and let that lease go to pot. Another company took it over and drilled a well on it and there was never a dry hole found on that 320 acres. It was the famous Teeter Pool. If I'd stayed home and run my oil company I'd have been a millionaire. But I always did let ethics beat me out of money and I suppose I always will.

When my furnishings store on 12th Street was about to blow up in 1922 it became time to nominate a judge of the county court for Jackson County from the Eastern District. Since I'd married I'd lived at Independence. It was thought that an ex-soldier was the right man for election. There were two factions in the county then and are yet, one called "goats" and one "rabbits." Back in 1914 my father had been a road overseer for the goat faction and when he died I had succeeded him. Then W. P. Borland the Congressman had appointed me Postmaster at Grandview, which job I held until the world war.

M. J. Pendergast came into my store one day and asked me if I'd like to run for Eastern judge. I told him I'd be delighted to do so. He didn't know I was busted. I ran and beat the rabbit candidate by some two or three hundred votes. Judge H. F. McElroy and I were elected as the majority of the County Court with a good old man by the name of E. W. Hayes, as Presiding Judge. Hayes was a rabbit. McElroy and I ran the Court and took all the jobs, so that in 1924 when we came up for reelection the "rabbits" scratched us both off the ticket and we were beaten along with the State ticket and all the balance of the Democratic ticket. I went to work for the Automobile Club of Kansas City and got them a thousand new members for which I received fifteen thousand dollars in commission. It cost me ten thousand dollars to do the job but I still had enough left for a living.

In the meantime Kansas City adopted a new Charter under the direction of the Republican Administration. When the city election came in 1926 the Democrats won by some 324 votes and Judge McElroy was made City Manager. When the fall elections came I was elected Presiding Judge of the County Court. The most distressing thing in the County at the time was its road system. There were miles and miles of water-bound macadam roads and they were being pounded to pieces much faster than they could be repaired. About this time the city (Kansas City) decided to ask for a bond issue to build new buildings, parks and boulevards and I suggested to my associates that we ask for enough money to build a road system. They agreed to it and we then employed a couple of outstanding engineers, Col. now Major General E. M. Stayton and N. T. Veatch, Jr., to outline a plan for us. Stayton is a Democrat and Veatch is a Republican. They drew up a fine plan costing $6,500,000.00 and it was submitted along with some $28,000,000.00 for Kansas City. The road bonds and some $250,000.00 of the City bonds carried.

The Court then employed Stayton and Veatch to carry out the road plan. It was carried out to the letter. No favorites for contracts were allowed and in 1931 when the City's Ten Year plan was voted the County received a vote of confidence for $3,500,000.00 more for roads and $4,200,000.00 for two new Court Houses, one in Independence and one in Kansas City.

When the last bond issue was voted I went to every city in the country except Los Angeles and Miami, Fla., where I could see the new civic buildings. It was decided that a colonial structure was proper for Independence at $200,000.00 and a semi-modern classical building would be proper for Kansas City. The Court insisted on having the best architects the City could produce for the creation of the plans and specifications and also hired the Architect of the best Court House plan in the country as consultant. The Architects were Keene and Simpson and Wight and Wight of Kansas City and Edward F. Neild of Shreveport, La., for consultant. The construction of these buildings was handled just as the construction of the county roads was. And now I am a candidate for the United States Senate. If the Almighty God decides that I go there I am going to pray as King Solomon did, for wisdom to do the job.

PART FIVE

The Man

I

WHENEVER THE President talks about government or people the word he uses most frequently is happiness. Happiness may be considered a quaint word today. But happiness does not mean welfare or security alone to Mr. Truman, nor does it mean the accumulation of wealth or honors, and it never means domination of other men.

The President said, "Happiness is a state of mind. A farmhand, if he has an ample living, can be just as happy as a millionaire with homes in Maine and Florida. Wealth is a relative proposition, but all men must be assured of an opportunity to work and then it's up to them. But happiness comes from contentment in doing what a man wants to do no matter what kind of work he is doing, provided he does not hurt his neighbor. A man must take pride in his work, but he must go on working because that is the life which gives him peace of mind. Governments are set up to bring about order and their end is to create happiness for men. But government is for all the people and not for any one group or for any special groups. The people have no lobby in Washington looking out for their interests except the President of the United States and it's too bad if the President does not work for their good."

Politics to the President means government.

The President continued.

"It is a pity that some people have a contemptuous idea of politics because politics under our system is government and a man who is not interested in politics is not doing his patriotic duty toward maintaining the constitution of the United States. I am proud to be a politician and to work politically for the happiness and the welfare of the country."

[195]

I asked the President what advice he would give to a young man who wanted to go into politics.

Mr. Truman said, "The first thing I would say to him is 'Go get yourself a first class education and then make yourself useful to all your neighbors. Become acquainted with everybody in your precinct. Then I would get to know something about law and banking and farming and how people work in factories and then spend my time learning how to get along with people.'

"But you have got to like people, and you will not be a good politician unless you *do* like people no matter how much you learn. You have got to want to help people, and you have got to help them not for your own benefit or welfare but for their happiness and welfare."

I asked the President what organizations a young man interested in politics should join, and he replied, "Well, being a joiner helps the politician. It helps to get around and see people. But you can soon tell a good politician by how sincere he is in liking and wanting to help people."

I asked the President to tell me how he had gotten into politics.

The President said, "When I became of voting age, I lived in a country precinct in a country township, and my father was road overseer and a leader in the community. At election time I was always the Democratic clerk helping count votes with the Republican clerk. That was in Grandview and I knew everybody in the whole surrounding territory, and was kin to most of them, so it wasn't too much trouble polling the precinct. There was one nice old man, a Socialist, who would come in and vote the Socialist ticket every time. There was a Republican judge, whose name was L. C. Hall, one of the best friends I ever had. He used to do all the threshing for us on the farm. And one time we had two Socialists votes, and when old man Hall came to tally the second vote he said: 'Harry, it looks like old man Green has voted twice. Do you reckon he did?' He hadn't, of course, because it was his son that had voted the Socialist ticket as well.

"Politics begins in the precincts. A young man who wants a political career must be willing to work wherever he can do the most good. If he can poll the precinct for his organization, he ought to do it. If the organization asks him to run for committee man, he ought to do it. I did, and I got licked the first time I ever ran for township committeeman. But I profited by my experience. I never had a political job that I wanted. But when it was my turn to fill out the Democratic ticket, I always got out and gave it everything I had, and I have never been defeated but once, and that was on account of a split in the Party at home in 1924."

I asked the President what he meant when he said he never wanted any of the public offices he held.

Mr. Truman replied, "I never ran for an office that I wanted to run for. When I ran for Presiding Judge I really wanted to be the County Collector. But I got outmaneuvered on that. Then when I completed eight years as Presiding Judge I wanted to run for Congress in a new district that had been set up in Missouri. But a judge of the circuit court wanted that position, and he outmaneuvered me, and I was asked to run for the Senate and I was elected as Senator.

"One rule that I did make in the beginning in politics was that I would have nothing to do with money. I just wouldn't handle it. I wouldn't collect it, I wouldn't distribute it, I wouldn't have anything in the world to do with it. And the boss politicians respected me because of this, although they never did understand it."

One evening at Blair House, I ventured the observation that some presidents seemed to appoint cabinet officers principally from their own state. The President smiled and said "Cronyism, the Missouri gang, you mean?"

The President continued: "I have never filled any key positions in the Cabinet with any former personal friends of mine, except the Secretary of the Treasury. Not a single darn one of them! I never saw Dean Acheson until he was either Under Secretary or Assistant Secretary of State. I never met Secretary of Commerce Sawyer until I met him as an Ambassador to Belgium on my way to Potsdam. Secretary of Defense Lovett was brought in by Marshall and I kept him because he is a good man.

"Brannan was a career man and I made him Secretary of Agriculture. Donaldson was a career man in the Post Office Department, and you know he started from the bottom there. Harriman, I inherited from Roosevelt, and he is an able and distinguished citizen who has done a whale of a job for me. The Secretary of the Interior, Oscar Chapman, is a career man I promoted after I had Krug for Secretary of Interior. And Tobin, Secretary of Labor, was Governor of Massachusetts when I first met him and he is a fine person and a good man.

"The one cabinet member I have from Missouri, although he really comes from Arkansas, is John Snyder. He was Defense Plants Director under Jesse Jones in the RFC. He became head of the Office of War Mobilization and Reconversion, succeeding Fred Vinson. When Vinson left the Treasury to become Chief Justice of the United States, John Snyder became Secretary of the Treasury. He had come right along, and he is capable and efficient, or I wouldn't have had him as Secretary of the Treasury."

At this point I interrupted the President to refer to his order of sweeping reorganization of the Bureau of Internal Revenue and the President's statement that this reorganization is "part of a program to prevent improper conduct in the public service, to protect the government from the insidious influence-peddlers and favor seekers, and to expose and punish any wrongdoers. It is one of a series of actions I am taking to insure honesty, integrity and fairness in the conduct of all government business."

The President said, "This is a policy I have always followed. It has never been anything else and I have never done it any other way. I had the same trouble in Jackson County. Whenever it became necessary, I fired people right and left. But I wouldn't let men be fired for an unjust purpose; they always had a fair chance to clear themselves."

He added, "I have gone around many a block to keep from hurting people, but sometimes I have had to do it."

I said, "You know, it is said about you, that you have stood by a man to the last drop of mercy."

Mr. Truman replied, "I would rather have that said about me than to be a great man."

I then asked the President about political bosses. He said, "Bosses are usually men who are interested in the political game, who are willing to put themselves out and do everything possible for people—accommodate them—really to have the welfare of their constituents at heart.

"But like all men, and just like every other outfit in politics, bosses go to seed. Take most politicians. They never get out until they die or are kicked out. And that happens to political bosses, too. When bosses get to the point where they have too much power, then they are dangerous. It is then that political bosses become a menace to politics and to people.

"But political bosses are part of the political system of the country. Tweed, head of the Tweed gang, was one of the first big political bosses. Then there was Charles Murphy, in New York City—who was in part a benevolent person, a friend of Al Smith and one who had made a contribution to his party.

"But when a political boss stays too long and gets too much power, then he is no longer benevolent. He is a danger."

The President went on about his favorite subject. "Politics is a fascinating game, because politics is government. It is the art of government.

"No man can sit here at this desk without feeling he is out of touch with the people unless he has come up from the grassroots or the precincts as a political worker. As a precinct worker he learns at first hand what the needs and problems of the people are.

"Take a very accomplished and brilliant man like John Quincy Adams, who was a fine ambassador and Secretary of State. When he became President, he seemed to be lost because he lacked that experience as an administrator or organizer who is in touch with the requirements of the people and for that reason he did not do as good a job as President."

II

Mr. Truman often says with dry humor that if he had been a good pianist he would never have been President of the United States.

As a boy, he used to get up at five o'clock in the morning to practice for two hours. He needed no urging from mother or teacher. He had ambitions in music.

How strangely the years and events have intervened since that time to this, as he sat playing the piano at Blair House one evening of reminiscence.

Mr. Truman still loves music as he does art and poetry and books, for all these mean living and happiness. The President is a self-educated man. His life has not permitted

 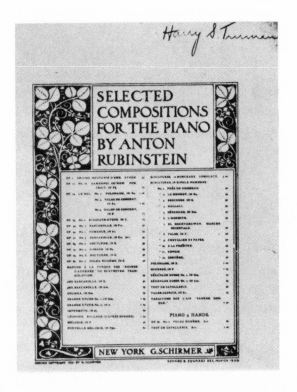

him the long years of study and practice needed for music, nor for college. He has sought to balance the scales against the things he has missed, and has probed more deeply into them than many who have had more time.

Architects are surprised at the President's knowledge in their field. As Presiding Judge, or head councilman, for a councilman is what a county judge is in Missouri, Mr. Truman supervised the building of the court house in Kansas City, Missouri. He made special trips around the country visiting court houses, and speaking to architects, before he approved the final plans and the design.

The President was and is an avid reader, and I have seen him even consulting reference books on geography and geology.

But music is his great love outside of politics.

His favorite composers are Mozart and Beethoven and Chopin. But he also loves the music of Florodora and the Strauss waltzes and Gershwin. He does not understand Shostakovich, and no political reason is involved, but he does like Debussy.

Perhaps in the singing career of his daughter, Margaret, he sees fulfillment of something of his own youthful dream.

He frequently obliges, for the fun of it, by playing a piece or two for his friends; but sometimes when alone he ventures a little more boldly. Today amidst the great pressure of events, it is easier for him to turn to good records for enjoyment and solace.

"I never had to be driven to practice," the President said, improvising on the piano as he talked. "Practicing was pleasure and not work and I wish I could have found more time for it. The first bit of composition I played was 'The Return of Spring' which my mother had played before me. Then I learned to play Mendelssohn's 'Songs without Words' and then pieces by Chopin and Von Weber and Jackson and Newland and one seldom hears of these last two now.

"I missed being a musician and the real and only reason I missed being one is because I wasn't good enough."

The President writing a friend about a year ago says about his music teacher, "Mrs. E. C. White, who was the wife of Professor White, the principal of Central High School and afterward superintendent of schools in Kansas City, lived at 27th and Brooklyn in a great, big old-fashioned brick house. I used to go up there once or twice a week and she gave me lessons on a fine old Steinway piano that she owned. I suppose you must have taken lessons on that same piano. She gave a recital once in a while and she always gave me a showy, brilliant piece to play. The mothers of her other pupils always said she played favorites with the boys—maybe she did."

I asked the President to tell me some of the compositions he liked; and improvising on

THE WHITE HOUSE
SOUTH VIEW

THE WHITE HOUSE
SIDE VIEW

the piano as he talked, he said, "Well, I am very fond of Mozart's Ninth Sonata, and the Scherzo by Mendelssohn. These are piano pieces. And then Beethoven's *Fifth Symphony* . . . and take this bit from one of Chopin's waltzes, which are great favorites of mine.

"Chopin's Opus 42, A-flat Waltz, and his 64 Series, Numbers 1, 2 and 3—they are wonderful. Number 2 is the one most everybody is familiar with. Then Von Weber composed some beautiful things—'Rondo Brilliante' and the 'Polka Brilliante.' Those are the things I studied when I was a kid and I am still fond of them. Then, of course, I am fond of some of the turn of the century comic operas, *The Belle of New York* and *The Spring Maid*—there are some lovely waltzes in those. And here is a piece that a great pianist used to play as an encore—Strauss' 'Blue Danube Waltz.' There is nothing more lovely than that.

"I like Bach, too—his preludes and fugues.

"But I don't like noise that passes for music today. Maybe I'm old-fashioned. I like something with a tune or melody to it."

The President then played some old marching and waltzing tunes, saying, "Here is the 'Black Hawk Waltz,' popular in 1846 when Lincoln was a captain in the army. He served in the Black Hawk War. And here is a tune called 'A March Over the Waves' written about the same time. . . . And here is a march from the Spanish American War, but I can't remember the name of it."

The President suddenly remembered a dramatic experience at the Potsdam Conference, when Stalin had brought some Russian ballet dancers and musicians to stage a concert for the Big Three, Truman, Churchill and Stalin and their staffs.

The President said, "I then decided to show them all what Americans could do. I heard there was a young man in the Army who played the piano well. His name is Eugene List. I sent for him and asked him to play my favorite Chopin waltz, Opus 42. He didn't have the score. We started to hunt all over Europe before we could find a score. We finally got it from Paris and I turned the pages for young List, he didn't have time to rehearse it in advance.

"Opus 42, I think, is Chopin's greatest waltz. I like them all and I don't count the posthumously published waltzes—I am not sure that he wrote them."

The President talked about the hymns and the songs he used to sing at home. At this point, he looked up at the painting above the piano, saying, "There is the handsomest man who ever lived in the White House—Franklin Pierce, the fourteenth President. This is not a great painting, of course."

The President has very decided tastes in painting, as in music. He speaks frequently of Rembrandt's "Descent from the Cross." His favorite painters are Holbein, Franz Hals, Rubens and Leonardo da Vinci. He likes Gilbert Stuart, portrait painter of Washington.

The President said, "Hanging in my office is a portrait of Benjamin Franklin, painted in 1770 by a collateral descendant of Cardinal Richelieu. Howard Chandler Christy calls it one of the great portraits. The painting was a gift of General de Gaulle to the White House.

"I love beautiful pictures, landscapes and portraits that look like people.

"We see enough of squalor. I think art is intended to lift the ideals of the people, not to pull them down."

The President likes only two statues in the nation's capital. "My favorite is Augustus Saint-Gaudens' statue 'Grief' in Rock Creek Cemetery. It is the Adams Memorial. Henry Adams never wanted it called 'Grief.' It is a memorial to his wife.

"And the statue of Lincoln in the Lincoln Memorial is wonderful.

"I think the finest horseback statue in this country is in Charlottesville, Virginia. It is the statue of Stonewall Jackson.

"I have been interested for years in equestrian statues. After viewing the work of many men when I was Presiding Judge of the Court, I selected Charles Keck to do the statue of Andrew Jackson which now stands in front of the court house in Kansas City, Missouri.

"It is interesting how much history you can learn by just studying statues and buildings. You know, if I couldn't have been a pianist, I think I would have done better as a professor of history."

I asked what incident in history or local expression had inspired that sentence in his recent press conference, "Wrongdoers have no house with me."

The President said, "It was inspired by a line in Romeo and Juliet. Shakespeare and the Bible are rich in expressions which men borrow from time to time."

I asked the President what books had influenced him the most and he replied, "The one that had the most influence is right here—the Holy Bible. Then Shakespeare.

"I always was a great reader. There was a little library in Independence, with some three or four thousand volumes in it—encyclopedias and histories and novels like those of George Eliot and Sir Walter Scott. From the time I was twelve I spent hours in the library and in reading the books I took out of the library including the encyclopedias—ain't that silly?"

There is a clue to the President's thinking in the copy of a poem which he carries around with him in his wallet.

"The statue of Andrew Jackson in Kansas City, Missouri, was made by Charles Keck, one of the great sculptors of this age. Charles Keck was asked to make the statue because I had seen his Stonewall Jackson statue at Charlottesville, Virginia, which is considered the finest equestrian statue in America. In making this statue of Andrew Jackson in Kansas City, Mr. Keck, Mr. Tom Wight, one of the architects of the court house and I went to 'The Hermitage,' measured his dress uniform and had the War Department furnish us with the equipment that was customary in 1814 for a general of the army. Mr. Keck very carefully looked at the beautiful marble bust of the General in 'The Hermitage' which is supposed to be the best likeness of him and also at the Ralph Earl portrait which is considered to be the best portrait of him. This statue in front of the Kansas City court house and the one on the east lawn of the court house in Independence, Missouri, I think are wonderful contributions to the equestrian statues of America."

The President said, "It's from *Locksley Hall*, by Alfred Tennyson. I've been carrying that ever since I graduated from high school."

I copied it out. Here it is:

> "For I dipt into the future, far as human eye could see,
> "Saw the Vision of the world, and all the wonder that would be;
> "Saw the heavens fill with commerce, argosies of magic sails,
> "Pilots of the purple twilight, dropping down with costly bales;
> "Heard the heavens fill with shouting, and there rain'd a ghastly dew
> "From the nations' airy navies grappling in the central blue;
> "Far along the world-wide whisper of the south-wind rushing warm,
> "With the standards of the peoples plunging thro' the thunder-storm;
> "Till the war-drum throbb'd no longer, and the battle-flags were furl'd
> "In the Parliament of Man, the Federation of the World.
> "There the common sense of most shall hold a fretful realm in awe,
> "And the kindly earth shall slumber, lapt in universal law."

III

President Truman says the President of the United States is five persons in one:

"He is the executive officer of the government. He is the leader of his party. He has certain legislative duties, consisting of signing bills or vetoing them. He is the social head of the state. And he is Commander in Chief of the armed forces."

A President cannot escape certain formalities, whatever his personal wishes; and people expect protocol in some ceremonial form, such as a flag or coat of arms.

Yet strange as it may seem, Mr. Truman is the first President to establish by executive order a legal definition of the President's Coat of Arms and his Seal. Up to 1945 there was no known basis in law for the coat of arms and the seal which had been used by Presidents since 1880 and which were reproduced on the flag. The seal had been originated during the administration of President Hayes, apparently as an erroneous rendering of the Great Seal of the United States.

The first President to have a presidential flag was Woodrow Wilson. Prior to that time the Army and Navy had separate flags for the Commander in Chief. Franklin D. Roosevelt, as Assistant Secretary of the Navy, and the Aide to the Secretary of the Navy, Commander Byron McCandless, U.S.N., designed a presidential flag which would be suitable for use by both the Army and the Navy.

WITH THE OLD PRESIDENTIAL STANDARD

President Truman said, "The flag consisted of a presidential coat of arms on a blue field with a white star in each of the corners. The coat of arms on the flag as well as on the seal showed an eagle facing to its own left toward the arrows gripped in one talon while in the right talon the eagle held an olive branch.

"I changed that. In the new coat of arms, seal and flag, the eagle not only faces to its right—the direction of honor—but also toward the olive branches of peace which it holds in its right talon. Formerly, as you know, the eagle faced toward the arrows in its left talon—arrows, symbolic of war."

Just before President Roosevelt died, he thought the four stars for the flag of the Commander in Chief were not appropriate, when there were five stars in the flags of the fleet admirals of the Navy and generals of the Army, grades which were created in December, 1944. Commander McCandless was asked to design a new flag and he sent a painting to the White House which proposed a flag with forty-eight stars.

But Mr. Truman had become President. Mr. Truman said, "I decided that the forty-eight stars should encircle the coat of arms in the Presidential flag and that the seal as well should show the forty-eight stars, representing the states collectively, no single star representing any particular state. The President is Commander in Chief but he is also the only direct representative of the people and therefore the forty-eight stars should represent all the people. I then issued an executive order setting the legal basis for the coat of arms, the seal and the flag.

"By the way, the old presidential flag and coat of arms had a white eagle. I asked that the American bald-headed eagle be put on the coat of arms, seal and flag."

The ceaseless curiosity of the President in details of this kind is again shown in his search for the origin of the ceremonial music that greets him whenever he appears at a public function, the strains of "Hail to the Chief."

Writing to the editor of the *People's Journal,* of Perth, Scotland, President Truman said, "A friend of mine has just sent me a clipping from your good paper of August sixth about the Scottish song, 'Hail to the Chief.' I am certainly happy to know the origin of the song." He asked for further information, wanting to know how the song had come to be used for presidential appearances.

The clipping has this headline: "It's a Scots Song that Greets Harry Truman." The news story reads:

" 'Hail to the Chief who in triumph advances' sing the men of Clan Alpine as they row their chief down Loch Katrine, a scene portrayed in 'The Lady of the Lake.'

"Now through some strange twist of history, the song is sung for a vastly greater chief than Roderick Dhu—no less a personage than the President of the U.S.A.

"Whenever he attends a public ceremony his arrival is heralded by the strains of 'Hail to the Chief.' The United States Marine Band alone plays the tune about 1000 times a year.

"A strange thing is that no one in the United States is sure how it became the Presidential theme song. Nearest anyone can get to it is that it was adopted in the early days of the Republic because of its title.

"In America it is practically a song without words, as these have been almost forgotten.

"The tune itself is said to come from an old Gaelic melody. The choral setting is by Sir Henry Rowley Bishop (1786-1855) who was engaged for three years as composer and director of the music at Covent Garden Theatre. The first work upon which he was employed was the music to 'The Knight of Snowdoun,' a musical drama founded on the Lady of the Lake. It was produced on February 5, 1811, and was acted 23 times."

Here is the song:

Hail to the Chief who in triumph advances!
Honoured and blessed be the ever-green pine!
Long may the tree, in his banner that glances,
Flourish, the shelter and grace of our line!
Heaven sent it happy dew,
Earth lend it sap anew;
Gaily to bourgeon and broadly to grow,
While every Highland glen
Sends our shout back agen,
"Roderigh Vich Alpine dhu, ho! ieroe!"

Ours is no sapling, chance-sown by the fountain,
Blooming at Beltane, in winter to fade;
When the whirlwind has stripped every leaf on the mountain,
The more shall Clan Alpine exult in her shade.
Moored in the rifted rock,
Proof to the tempest's shock,
Firmer he roots him the ruder it blow;
Menteith and Breadalbane, then,
Echo his praise agen,
"Roderigh Vich Alpine dhu, ho! ieroe!"

Proudly our pibroch has thrilled in Glen Fruin,
And Banochar's groans to our slogan replied;
Glen Luss and Ross-dhu, they are smoking in ruin,
And the best of Loch Lomond lie dead on her side.
Widow and Saxon maid
Long shall lament our raid,
Think of Clan Alpine with fear and with woe;
Lennox and Leven glen
Shake when they hear agen,
"Roderigh Vich Alpine dhu, ho! ieroe!"

Row, vassals, row, for the pride of the Highlands!
Stretch to your oars for the ever-green pine!
O! that the rosebud that graces yon islands
Were wreathed in a garland around him to twine!

O! that some seedling gem,
Worthy such noble stem
Honoured and blessed in their shadow might grow!
Loud should Clan Alpine then
Ring from her deepmost glen,
"Roderigh Vich Alpine dhu, ho! ieroe!"

The *People's Journal* added:

"It is still an intriguing mystery (this newspaper is dated October 8, 1949) why a song from the 'Lady of the Lake' is now the personal 'anthem' of the President.

"If any reader can throw light upon it, the Editor will be glad to pass it on to President Truman. . . . Sir Henry Bishop wrote many songs which are still popular, and President Truman will be interested to know that it is believed Bishop provided the setting of 'Home Sweet Home,' the words of which were by John Howard Payne, a New York actor, who became an American Consul."

This mystery still remains a mystery, so far as President Truman knows, but he thinks it's a wonderful tune and song.

IV

The President is a tireless collector of stories of the White House. Writing a friend he said:

"I can't tell you how very much I appreciate the description of Van Buren's rehabilitation of the White House. It is just exactly what I want to complete my historical file on what happened at the White House. I am trying to find a record of what Chester Arthur did to the White House when he became President after Garfield was shot. There is a story around here that he took all the old furniture out of the house, put it in the yard and held an auction—the furniture therefore is scattered from one end of the country to the other. Some of that old furniture was what had been purchased by Monroe and Jefferson in Paris.

"I found four chairs that Lincoln used for his Cabinet meetings piled up in the attic of the Treasury with broken legs and the upholstery all mouse eaten. I had the chairs restored, placed them in the Lincoln room and will put them back there when the house is finished."

AN EARLY DRAWING OF THE WHITE HOUSE

V

Since the purpose of this book is to show the mind of a man and not to write a final history, I think it would be helpful to give the following samples of the President's thoughts and interests as shown in some of his correspondence. It seems to me that they illustrate not only the mind of a President, and of Mr. Truman, the Man, but the world as it is today and the state of the union.

Years 1945-1946

Memorandum for: James F. Byrnes, Secretary of State

Mr. Edward R. Stettinius was in and discussed his personal plans, which are to go to the hospital for an operation. I think he discussed them with you.

Mr. Stettinius recommended that Adlai Stevenson act in his absence during preparatory stage in London. He said this met with your approval.

He also recommended the postponement of the meeting of the General Assembly be agreed to, and that it meet in January instead of December. He also said that met with your approval.

I told him I did not want to take a hand in the discussion for a permanent site for the organization—that should be decided by the organization itself—because I couldn't take sides for one city in the United States against all the rest.

———

The President's desk was damaged by fire in one of the drawers during the early part of President Roosevelt's first administration and he was presented with an inlaid mahogany desk, which I sent to Hyde Park.

The desk at which I sit has been the President's desk since the time of Theodore Roosevelt. Every President since has used it and I shall continue to use it.

———

Of course, you must remember, Germany is a conquered enemy country and I don't think there is any reason for giving them any special privileges. In fact it is the policy to see to it that Germany gets no better treatment than our Allies, which she ruined.

We are spending a great deal of time trying to get a stabilized Government in Germany and we are also doing everything we possibly can to alleviate the suffering in the countries which Germany devastated.

———

I think you are unduly agitated. I am most interested in a peace settlement that will work —I am not cramming anything down the throat of an independent nation that will interfere with that peace settlement.

———

I know that Japan is a terribly cruel nation in warfare but I can't bring myself to believe that, because they are cruel, we should ourselves act in the same manner. For myself, I certainly regret the necessity of wiping out whole populations because of the "pigheadedness"

nomination for Vice President. Finally
Mr. Hannegan, the Chairman of the
National Democratic Committee
called the President in San Diego.
Calif. He asked Mr. Hannegan if he
had recieved a commitment from
the Junior Senator from Missouri. Mr.
Hannegan told the President that he
had never been in contact with as
mulish and contrary a man. Then
the President said, and I could hear
him, "Well if he wants to let the
Democratic Party and the country
down in the midst of a war that's
his responsibility."
I was, to put it mildly ~~stunned.~~

WITH JOSEPH H. SHORT, PRESIDENTIAL PRESS SECRETARY

of the leaders of a nation and, for your information, I am not going to do it unless it becomes absolutely necessary. My object is to save as many American lives as possible but I also have a humane feeling for the women and children in Japan.

Year 1947

I took a walk this morning at a quarter of seven and passed that Zero Milestone twice. It is just across the street from the south portico of the White House. There is a baseball diamond just south of it and I get out field glasses and watch the games going on there. I tried once to go personally and witness one of these games and all I succeeded in doing was breaking it up.

As always, I am just trying to do the job I am supposed to do, and a lot of times, in public service, that is an unusual procedure, so it causes comment.

I can't go along with the setting-up of a supergovernment outside the control of both the Congress and the President no matter what good purpose it may serve.

You can rest assured that, as long as I am President, the gentlemen in Wall Street are not to control the operations of the International Bank.

There are two schools of thought on the pronunciation of the state from which I come. Most of us who live along the Missouri River pronounce it with the "i" just as you did. Some of our deep southern sections in southeast and south Missouri use the "a." In the old days the word with the "a" ending was sometimes used as the first name for a young lady.

You have been in politics long enough to know that there are a number of people who are always doing things for the ones who hold public office. Somebody is always doing something in the name of the Governor of Missouri or the President of the United States and, in a great many instances, the public officials are not consulted.

———

You remember one day informing me that a President had to have certain qualities which were not agreeble sometimes to his friends and that he had to be an unprintable man about half the time. I suppose you will think I have started exercising that prerogative on you, but that is not the case. I have been working at it now for about a year and I find it works out very well sometimes, although it does not make me very happy to have to play that way with my friends.

———

We are not going to relax the anti-trust laws as long as I am President.

———

Now don't get it into your head I have a "Palace Guard"—I haven't.

———

I can't agree that because Russia violates treaties we should follow her example and do the same thing.

———

Year 1948

Unless we can succeed in getting an economic recovery in Europe we might just as well look forward to a real dark age because where Russia gets control the standard of living goes back a thousand years—at least that has happened in nearly every one of the satellite countries.

———

There are some two hundred and forty million people on this side of the iron curtain who are anxious to maintain free governments, as we understand the term. Should we fail in their support now, there will be a tremendous bill to pay sometime in the next twenty-five years. I've done everything I can to get a peaceful settlement of this situation.

Your friend, of course, is not familiar with all the details entering into the world situation. Agreements which were made long before I came to the White House and which had to be carried out in order to finish up the war, also had to be carried out in the hope that they would result in a satisfactory peace settlement. To date, that hasn't happened.

———

When you get an education, that is something nobody can take from you—money is only temporary—but what you have in your head, if you have the right kind of a head, stays with you.

———

The nomination of Dewey last night I think will make the campaign easier—all he can do is to make a "warmed-over" approach to the situation with which the country is faced and I don't think the country is going to take a "warmed-over" approach.

———

There is a lot of conversation about a meeting between Stalin and me and I have always said that if Stalin wants to come to Washington and visit the United States I would be glad to see him, but I can't see where anything would be gained by a conversation with him.

———

I have never seen the irritable, petulant and angry President—you probably have been reading certain columnists—they are not really reliable reporters, you know.

———

I am sorry that you are not friendly with General Marshall. He will probably go down in history as one of the great men of our era, not because he was the chief military brains in winning the war, but because he is also a great statesman and a diplomat.

———

I was working at the National Bank of Commerce in 1903 during the great flood and, at that time, we were living at 2108 Park Avenue in Kansas City—my old red-haired grandmother was living with us. We took her down to see this flood, because she had seen the famous one of 1844, and she said the 1903 flood looked a lot bigger to her than the 1844 flood did, although it was checked at two feet below the 1844 record.

———

I was very glad to have an opportunity to talk to you and try to explain to you that the Russian situation is one of Russia's own making. We have put forth every effort possible to get a peace by negotiation and, as I told you on that day, the Russians have not only not kept their agreements but they have obstructed the approach in the United Nations, which would cure the thing and they are still doing just that. All we can do is to keep trying.

———

We must keep trying for peace. The false approach of the Russians must not prevent our peace program from going through to a successful conclusion.

———

The President of the United States has to be very careful not to be emotional or to forget that he is working for one hundred and forty-five millions people primarily, and for peace in the world as his next objective.

———

If the Republicans continue to perform as they have, I don't think there is any doubt in the world but what we will win.

———

I fear very much that your analysis of the situation is somewhat biased by your connections. I am sure that right down in your heart you know that the ordinary man is the backbone of any country—particularly is that true in a republic and what I am trying to eliminate is the fringe at each end of the situation. I think small business, the small farmer, the small corporations are the backbone of any free society and when there are too many people on relief and too few people at the top who control the wealth of the country then we must look out. We are not in that situation and we are not going to get there as long as I am President of the United States if I can prevent it. I expect to give everybody, big and little, a fair deal and nothing less.

———————

I am not in favor of erecting memorials to people who are living. I think it is bad business because a person may do something before he dies that will make the people want to tear the memorial down.

———————

Year 1949

I am exceedingly proud of the fact that I appointed the first Puerto Rican to be governor of that lovely Island and that I was President when the first elected Governor was inaugurated.

It is my ambition to make this Republic of ours stand for predominant self-government everywhere in the world and I think we have followed that procedure when you remember the conditions of the Spanish Colonies in 1898.

Cuba, Puerto Rico and the Philippines are all self-governing entities now and I sincerely hope that the citizens and people of Puerto Rico will always want to remain citizens of the United States. I rather think they will, although it is their decision as to whether they will or not.

———————

I am not, and never have been, in favor of absentee landlordism in our farm program. One of the difficulties with which we are faced in this machine age is to keep the farms in the hands of owners and occupiers of the land.

There is a tendency all over the country to create large blocks of acreage operated by machines in the hands of hired men. I don't believe in it. I think the greatest asset this country has always had has been landownership by small holders both in the country and in the cities and I think if you will analyze it you will agree with me on this subject.

———————

One of the main difficulties we must overcome is the difficulty to get people in administrative places who do not drag their feet on the carrying out of a program.

We have one immense difficulty in the Congress for the simple reason that seniority creates power in that legislative body and seniority means that men of the previous generation are in control of the key committees. There seems to be no remedy for this situation due to the fact that a contest for chairmanships would create so much bitterness that business could not be transacted at all. I won't say that all the old men are looking backward—we have some very able and distinguished liberals who have been in Congress a long time—the Vice-President is one of them, as is Sam Rayburn, the Speaker of the House.

———

I appreciate very much your note to Matt Connelly, enclosing him a tally sheet from the 2nd and 3rd Wards of Kansas City, back in 1926. That certainly is an interesting document. My county majority in that race was sixteen thousand; four years later it was fifty-five thousand and four years later it was one hundred and forty-two thousand, so you can see there was general improvement as time went along.

———

I appreciated very much your letter of the twentieth. It is the honest frankness of real friends that helps a man improve his delivery over the radio. I don't think there is anybody in the country who had as rotten a delivery as I did to begin with but thanks to good friends like you, who have been honestly helpful in their criticism, I think there has been some improvement.

———

I received a card the other day from Steve Early which said, "Don't Worry Me—I am an 8 Ulcer Man on 4 Ulcer Pay."

———

I was reading a story in one of the papers the other day where a man had called the doctor about 3 o'clock in the morning and said that his wife had appendicitis and that he wished the doctor would come immediately and do something about it. The doctor told the man to give his wife carbonate of soda—that he knew very well that she didn't have two appendixes as he had taken one out just three years before. The man came back with the statement that he knew a woman couldn't have two appendixes but a man could have two wives in three years.

———

The people who are responsible for the operation of the Government are entirely under-paid and I sincerely hope that the adjustment of their pay will be passed by the Senate and the House without undue delay.

The general run of employees have had two special raises in the last two years and there are instances where the heads of the departments, who are responsible to the President, receive less pay than their chief clerks. You can hardly expect to run an organization and keep the morale up when that is the case.

———

Those of us who were born and brought up in Missouri are braggarts when it comes to talking about that state, and I wouldn't dare start outlining to you just a few of the things for which that old state is famous.

You know there has been an immense amount of argument as to what the name itself means. I don't know whether you have followed it or not, but we have finally come to the conclusion that it doesn't mean "Big Muddy" but "A River of Wooden Boats." There are several other translations of the Indian term which sound nothing like the English spelling but I dare not go into that because I would create a long-winded controversy which is of no value.

———

The Government of the United States has tried to exercise circumspection in the settlement of affairs after the second World War. Your survey of the situation gives me a great deal of pleasure because all we are anxious to attain is a peaceful world in which all nations can live as they choose and freely exchange commodities and ideas with each other.

Naturally we have all been disappointed by the attitude of the Russians. I tried for more than two years to reach an understanding with them but that is an impossibility unless the Russians know they can't run over the rest of the world. I believe we are well on the road to attaining that position, and then I am sure we will have a settlement that will be fair and just to everybody.

———

I must look up that American history by W. E. Woodward. I also have been doing some reading on the Spanish Conquistadors and the trek of Coronado from Mexico City to eastern Kansas. As you know, they have on several occasions unearthed Spanish sabers and pieces of armor as far east as Shawnee just outside of Kansas City.

———

Your letter of April first is most interesting. The main difficulty is that you start off with the wrong premise. Nobody is working for socialized medicine—all my Health Program calls for is an insurance plan that will enable people to pay doctor bills and receive hospital treatment when they need it.

I can't understand the rabid approach of the American Medical Association—they have distorted and misrepresented the whole program so that it will be necessary for me to go out and tell the people just exactly what we are asking for.

I am trying to fix it so the people in the middle income bracket can live as long as the very rich and very poor.

I am glad you wrote me because I think there are a lot of people like you who need straightening out on this subject.

———————

I think what we need more than anything else in the educational field is the proper training of teachers. I don't think it makes any difference about vocational training, school buildings or anything else if we get the proper psychological training among our teachers. Next to a mother the teacher has more influence on a child than any other person in the country and what I am after is a proper approach to the teacher program.

———————

We don't play halfway politics in Missouri. When we start out with a man, if he is any good at all, we always stay with him to the end. Sometimes people quit me but I never quit people when I start to back them up.

———————

It is much better to go down fighting for what is right than to compromise your principles.

———————

We have killed and injured more people on the road since the automobile came in than were killed and injured in all the wars we ever fought from the Revolution on. We have a useless waste of life with unnecessary fires. We have more industrial accidents than we care to enumerate and after the showing we made in two world wars with the help of the young people, I've been endeavoring to meet all these situations at the source. We have more than twenty-six million disabled people as the result of these unnecessary accidents—most of the injured absolutely dependent either on their families or charity.

The draft showed that more than thirty-four per cent of our young men and women were physically unfit for service—that percentage is too great—we must do something about it if we expect this great Republic to continue in the future.

———

Copy of a quotation on my desk at the White House—

"Always do right. This will gratify some people, & astonish the rest.

Truly yours, Mark Twain

New York Feb. 16, 1901"

A good sentiment.

/s/ Harry S. Truman

———

Year 1950

Political rumors such as this are bound to go around in election year. You and I have been in the game long enough to know that they usually have no foundation in fact. Whenever I get ready to fall out with a man I tell him first and not the rumormongers.

———

It has always been my opinion that those who profit most from the government expenditures should pay most for the support of the government.

———

These politicians who make agreements and then find excuses for not keeping them are something like the Russians. When they make agreements they make them only to break them.

———

As to Point IV, it is not intended to be a money-spending program from the viewpoint of the Federal Government. What I am proposing in Point IV is technical assistance, which we will furnish at a comparatively small expense and then I am hoping that our immense pool of idle capital can be invested in such a manner as to improve the economic conditions of countries with immense resources and no capital to develop them.

Point IV is not another ECA program—it is I hope a common-sense approach to world development in such a way as to keep our own country prosperous and to improve the living standards of those people who have immense resources in their countries and because they are undeveloped have a low standard of living.

———

You are advocating just exactly what the United States was formed to prevent. The free nations of the world have a perfect right to attend to their own affairs in any manner they see fit.

———

MARK TWAIN

Don't spend a lot of money on advertising. Political advertising just doesn't bring in the votes. Handshakes before election day and precinct workers on that day to see that the voters come to the polls win elections.

———

I rather think there is an immense shortage of Christian charity among so-called Christians.

No President ever can tell what the best approach to world affairs is. He has to use his best judgment and try to keep things on an even keel for the welfare of his own country. Any schoolboy can tell him what he should have done, after the fact is accomplished.

I shall continue to do what I think is right whether anybody likes it or not.

There is nothing in the world that boy couldn't have had if he had just had a teaspoonful of common sense.

I hope everything is going well with you and I also hope the next time you see Jerome you will speak to him in the same restrained manner that a sergeant talks to a mule.

I can't do that, however, because a commitment has already been made on that appointment. Anyway I don't like maneuvers like that and I really don't think you do either, if you will think it through. When such things are done it gives the politicians who comply with them a bad name and, as you know, in my book the profession of politics is the highest and most important business in the world.

I like to do things in a fair and square way with all the cards on the table and I am sure that you understand even if a commitment had not been made I would not even consider a maneuver such as you suggest.

The only reason I am answering your letter at all is because you have always been a friend of mine and I don't like to see my friends go wrong.

A Federal judge, particularly the district judges, comes in closer contact with the people than any other part of the Federal Government. If a man is assured of a fair and impartial trial he knows his interests are properly protected and that the Republic is safe.

I think our Constitution and its Bill of Rights is the greatest document of government in the history of the world and I am doing my best to contribute my share to upholding it.

"Youth, the Hope of the World." That was the motto on the High School front door from which I graduated, only it was written—"Juventus Spes Mundi."

If you will remember, General MacArthur was made Allied Commander of the Occupation Forces in Japan by me, at which time I forced an agreement out of the Russians to accept him in that position.

His latest appointment, Commander in Chief, United Nations Command, was made by me at the suggestion of the United Nations. The United Nations didn't suggest him—they suggested to me that I appoint the Allied Commander and I appointed MacArthur.

I am going to spend the rest of my life in an endeavor to cause a return to truthful writing and reporting.

Men often mistake notoriety for fame, and would rather be remarked for their vices and follies than not be noticed at all!

I don't know what gets into the heads of you "liberals" who think that the man who sets the policies is going to change his mind with every change of the moon. I announced the policy I proposed to follow, September 6, 1945, and there has been a continuous effort to implement that policy with a continually hostile Congress, no matter what it was called, and I think we have succeeded right well in getting many things done that were contemplated in that message. To it we have added a Peace Program known as Point Four and a Health Program, both of which will eventually accomplish the purpose for which they are intended.

It looks as if woman suffrage didn't create the interest in government that everybody thought it would. Then I think a great many people have come to the conclusion that an interest in politics is a disgraceful procedure. Most of them do not understand that politics is government and that when they refuse to take an interest in local political affairs they are unpatriotic.

I hope we can cure that frame of mind by a sincere effort to restore an interest in the right to vote.

———

My grandfather, Solomon Young, was in the freighting business in a big way from Westport to Salt Lake City and San Francisco between 1846 and 1860. He made at least a dozen round trips and was one of the big freighters at the time. You will find a most interesting record about one of his trips in the archives of the Mormon Church in Salt Lake City. On his first trip with his own Bills of Lading the consignee who happened to be the United States Government at Salt Lake City refused to accept the goods because the colonel in charge wanted another freighter to haul them. My grandfather made a deal with Brigham Young and came out whole on the matter. That is a matter of record in the Church files now.

———

I have had personal contact with mustard gas, with chlorine and with phosgene in the field and, just between you and me and the gatepost, I don't like any of them. There is an international agreement against the use of gas in warfare and I am for it one hundred per cent. I just can't bring myself to sponsor the use of gas in warfare.

———

You know most everybody understands just exactly what to do on a battlefield and can tell the commanding general about what he should do. That has been the case ever since Hannibal invaded Italy but when you get right down to brass tacks the man in the field is the one who has to make the decision. Therefore, he has to have a lot of leeway from his commander back home.

———

I was in Paris when President Wilson arrived after World War I. I was starting on leave from the front. I don't think I ever saw such an ovation as he received. It certainly is too bad that Wilson's part of the Versailles Treaty was not approvd.

———

I was intrigued by your description of the farewell tour of Weber and Fields, Lillian Russell and Nat Wills. I was working in a bank at Kansas City at that time and they appeared at the old Convention Hall. I've never seen a better show and I don't think I ever will see a better one because I was at the age when things of that sort make an impression. It was my privilege to see the four Cohens when they were at the height of their popularity, Eva Tanguay and the first tour of Florodora when it had the original sextette. I've often wondered why there couldn't be a revival of some of those great musical shows of the early 1900s. There was the Spring Maid, the Girl from Utah, the Pink Lady and the Belle of New York. I think they would be just as good today as they were when you and I were in our teens.

Year 1951

One of the difficulties from which this country is likely to suffer is that some seem to think that everything ought to be handed to them on a silver platter without any effort on their part. When a nation ceases to have something to struggle for it usually gets fat and dies of a heart ailment just like a human being does.

———

I have several histories of Russia—not one of which has been satisfactory. Most of them are based on ideas that were formed before the man started his book and are not based on facts. I think it is up to us to find out all we can about the inside of Russia and then act accordingly.

———

No officer ought to be given the responsibility of the lives of the men under him unless he is capable and competent—I don't care what the color of his skin is.

———

I know how you feel when you want to punch some old backward-looking fellow in the nose because he can't see the necessity for what has to take place.

———

Editors are peculiar animals—they throw mud and bricks at you the whole year round—then they make one favorable statement which happens to agree with facts and they think they should be hugged and kissed for it.

———

I don't know what my situation will be in April 1952, but you might write me a letter two or three weeks ahead of the date and I can then come nearer giving you a definite answer. I am not my own boss any more, as you know—I am the hired man of one hundred and fifty million people and it is a job that keeps me right busy.

———

THE LINCOLN MEMORIAL

I think one of the reasons for the lack of interest in the right to vote is fundamentally due to plain laziness and the idea of letting George do it. Voters who claim they have no hand in the selection of candidates or those who take no interest in the political party are like a great many people who do not like to take responsibility themselves but who find it much more pleasant to find fault with those who are willing to take the responsibility.

———

His viewpoint is almost opposite to mine but you must understand that sixteen years ago Burt Wheeler was one of the few Senators in the Senate who was in any way decent to the Junior Senator from Missouri and I can't forget that. That doesn't necessarily mean that he has any influence with me as to policy but I shall continue to like him as long as I live.

———

Everybody needs to get away once in a while and take a look at things a thousand miles from Washington. The country is entirely different even forty miles away than it is in the Merry-Go-Round that we have to ride all the time.

———

As you know, all I want is world peace and we can't obtain world peace by saber rattling or by the efforts of someone in high command to involve us in a third world war. I tried my best to explain our policy and program last night in my statement to the nation. I am enclosing you a copy of it.

We cannot overlook the fact that this country now must have technicians and experts who know their jobs. I've been thinking seriously about suggesting that we establish an engineering and technical expert school on the order of West Point and Annapolis for the purpose of educating technical men for the use of the Government.

I can remember on the farm in Missouri when I was a very small child how my mother and grandmother worked over the sausage and the rendering of the lard. They had a recipe for rendering lard that caused it to become just as white as snow and to keep forever. They stored it in large tin cans and fixed some of the sausage as you fixed it, in those two jars you sent me, and then they would put the rest of it in sacks and smoke it with the hams and bacon. When I went back to the farm in 1906 we carried on the hog killing time just as our grandparents had done it, but it is a lost art now.

I appreciated your letter of the eighteenth very much and, of course, I know about Jefferson and Franklin being branded "Socialists." Their socialism was for the welfare of the common everyday man and that is what we are accomplishing in these days. It has taken a century and a half even to approach the ideals of Jefferson and Franklin but perhaps in another century and a half we will have obtained the objective.

I appreciated very much yours of December eighteenth with the enclosure. I read with a lot of interest the "Moral Breakdown in Public Life." I think you will find that moral breakdown in public life is nothing new. It has been one of the fights that a republic has to make continually. Eventually we will win because the vast majority of the people and the vast majority of government employees are honest men.

SCENE DURING REMODELING OF WHITE HOUSE, 1951

As you say, complacency is our greatest weakness and always has been. Another situation with which we are faced that causes much difficulty, is the fact that every four years we go into a spasm of imaginary situations and lead the world to believe that we are irresponsible and cannot follow through.

Since nineteen hundred and thirty-nine we have pursued a straight policy in foreign affairs and I hope that policy can be continued on to a successful conclusion.

THE EMANCIPATION PROCLAMATION

PART SIX

The President Speaks of the Future

I

The President often says that we want for others what we want for ourselves, "and that is to live in peace and freedom."

He says:

"I should like even the humblest men in the remotest corners of the world, especially where people are now torn by hunger, and strife of revolution, and fanaticism and totalitarianism, to understand what we are trying to do. All we are trying to do is to encourage development of the earth's resources for the benefit of men everywhere."

I asked the President, "What would you say to the people of Russia or China, if you had an opportunity to address them directly?"

The President said:

"I have often wished and prayed for just such an opportunity.

"The first thing I would say is that we have no desire nor are we trying to change the world to fit the pattern of our own country. People everywhere express themselves and live their own lives in terms of their own background and culture, and that is their God-given right, as long as they do not attempt to impose by force or intrigue their ideas on their neighbors.

"We in America have waged many bitter struggles to preserve our freedom.

"This freedom has enabled our masses of people to enjoy an ever improved standard of living, free from the kind of toil that still is breaking the backs of hundreds of millions of people. I would offer American experience, American skill and American science to help lift the load from these people's backs. Many people who still live in the feudal ages are being hoodwinked by devilish propaganda today into false paradises.

"I would say beware of totalitarians who talk about democracy and peace. They have destroyed the real meaning of the words democracy and peace. They are world conspirators trying to substitute collective fanaticism and servitude for individual freedom.

"If I could speak to the Russian people, I would have this especially and specifically to say to them:

" 'Do NOT be misled by anyone to believe that you are in danger of being attacked by any nation west or east or south or north of your frontiers.

" 'Do not let yourselves be plunged helplessly into war as were the German people and the Italians and the Japanese.

" 'Do not let the Communist and Chinese aggression in Korea be used as a pretext for burdening you with further armaments that will cause you to live in a state of constant fear.

" 'Only your rulers can dispel your fears.

" 'With your resources fully developed for peaceful purposes, you could enjoy a better and more comfortable life.

" 'If your government ever gave any believable evidence by acts and performances that it is ready to cooperate with other nations within the United Nations to secure the peace then you could begin to reap the benefits of a world cooperating to improve the lot of mankind.

" 'In a world of cooperation we could easily undertake to show you that your vast resources can support in comfort 400 million people instead of 200 million without resorting to imperialistic exploitation of other countries.' "

II

The President says:

"I hate war. War destroys individuals and whole generations. It throws civilization into the dark ages. But there is only one kind of war the American people have any stomach for and that is war against hunger and pestilence and disease. Much as we have contributed to industrial and economic development, we have gotten even greater know-how in the saving and prolonging of human lives.

"We are the descendants of many peoples and nations. It is instinct for Americans to want to help their neighbors. We want neighbors to thrive and prosper. It is our policy to share our know-how and experts, our doctors and nurses. They constitute a kind of army

WITH SECRETARY OF DEFENSE ROBERT A. LOVETT

in white—an army of lifesavers—such as we have in this country and such as we ought to have in even greater strength.

"Doctors and nurses and technicians, equipped with those wonder drugs that we have learned to mass produce, could do much to clear the way for self-development of nations now being held back by hunger and disease."

III

The President has no patience with people who talk about "a preventive war."

"There are a few misguided people who want war to straighten out the present world situation," the President said. "But fortunately these people are a very small even though vocal minority, and they have no power.

"War is the most awful approach to the present problem that could possibly be made.

"It is not war that is going to solve this thing, but morals and ideas.

"I hope some day the simple creed of doing unto others as you would be done by will be the rule of the world. We must encourage that sort of thinking.

"And we need ideas to rebuild a world for peace, fresh ideas of cooperation to make the world more productive and a better place for men everywhere to live.

"We need ideas to combat those of the Communists. There is no such thing as communism in existence today, because it won't work. There is no communism in Russia. It is totalitarianism. Wherever you have thought control and complete subservience to a man or group of men with no civilian checks on their powers, then you have totalitarianism. Totalitarianism crushes freedom."

IV

Discussing war and peace one evening at Blair House, the President said:

"The human race has been striving for peace ever since civilization started. The United Nations represents the greatest organized attempt in the history of men to solve their differences without war.

"When two people disagree they try to negotiate or go to court for settlement.

"If we can get through this period of the cold war and the difficulty with the totalitarian states, we will eventually wind up with a world organization where we can settle things by negotiations or in the courts instead of with bayonets.

"The proposition is really simple. Take what happens in this country. We have a federal union of forty-eight states. Yet disputes may exist today between individual states of the union no matter how strong federal sovereignty is. One state may sue another state and go to court. Or states may enter into compacts with one another apart from their legal relations as parts of the United States.

"Take, for instance, the dispute that existed between Colorado and Kansas over the Arkansas River. If these states had been free and independent countries with no way of going to court or reaching a compact within the framework of the federal union, they would have gone to war.

"But Colorado and Kansas, with the consent of the United States Congress, agreed to settle their differences by a compact in 1949. Article One of this compact stated that its purpose was to 'settle existing disputes and remove causes of future controversy between the states of Colorado and Kansas, and between citizens of one and citizens of the other state, concerning the waters of the Arkansas River and their control, conservation and utilization for irrigation and other beneficial purposes.'

"Recently I signed an act of Congress granting authority to Louisiana and Texas to make a compact providing for an equitable apportionment of the waters of the Sabine River

"These compacts in no way weaken the sovereignty of the federal union nor the sovereignty which the Constitution safeguards for the individual states.

"It took eighty years to implement the government of the United States so that it would work.

"The aim of the United Nations is to substitute peaceful negotiations for war. We must make the United Nations grow in legal and moral strength as an instrument of world peace and order, remembering our experience and difficulties and growth as a federal union."

V

The President said:

"Ever since the end of World War II, the whole objective of my connection with the atomic setup has been to find the way to apply atomic energy to peaceful purposes. Atomic energy can be the greatest asset to civilization. We are harnessing it for peace and we do not intend to let it destroy us.

"There have been destructive inventions in the past that have been turned to constructive purposes, like dynamite and TNT. But these are toys compared to the power opened to us by the splitting of the atom.

"Experiments are now going on to find a way to use atomic energy as a source of power. Further experiments are being conducted of importance in a number of other fields but I cannot discuss them at this time.

"The British, who have a fuel problem, are making great strides in utilizing atomic energy for heating purposes.

"Before 1940, the British spent many millions trying to split the atom and then turned over the whole project completely to us when they found they did not have the resources to conclude their experiments and because Britain was not a safe haven against air raids. We followed through and were successful.

"Ever since the cessation of hostilities I have had the Atomic Energy Commission busy seeking peacetime uses of the immense energy released by the splitting of atoms.

"While we are pursuing with full zeal the development of atomic energy as a weapon we are working with equal zeal on its application for peaceful purposes."

I asked the President if he could tell me something of the events and factors that led him to make the decision to use the atomic bomb.

The President said:

"I first learned about our vast project of atom splitting about two weeks after I became President.

"While a Senator and chairman of the special committee to investigate the national defense program, I had come across an important project, the details of which were hard to ascertain. I sent a special investigator to look into the matter. Secretary of War Stimson then informed me that the project involved a topmost secret. I immediately called off the investigator, and said I did not want to know anything more about it.

"The secret was disclosed to me as President by James F. Byrnes, who had been Director of War Mobilization under President Roosevelt, and Fred M. Vinson, who had succeeded Byrnes. On April 25th, Secretary of War Stimson went over the whole project with me.

"President Roosevelt had initiated the project, its primary aim being the use of atomic energy for military purposes. The objective of the huge expenditure was to be the first to develop an atomic weapon and to use it. The Germans were trying to create such a weapon.

"On July 6th I left for the Potsdam Conference to meet with Churchill and Stalin. While at Potsdam I received a message saying that the scientists had made a successful test at Los Alamos, New Mexico, on July 16th.

"I went into immediate consultation with Byrnes, Stimson, Admiral Leahy, General Marshall, General Arnold, General Eisenhower and Admiral King. I asked for their opinions whether the bomb should be used. The consensus of opinion was that the bomb should be used.

"We were planning an invasion of Japan with the use of 2,000,000 men and the military had estimated the invasion might result in very heavy casualties. In April I had appointed an interim committee to make recommendations on questions of policy when and if an atomic bomb could be made. The Committee consisted of Secretary Stimson, George L. Harrison, James H. Byrnes, William L. Clayton, Dr. Vannevar Bush, Dr. Karl T. Compton, and Dr. James B. Conant. Before I had left for Potsdam the committee had recommended that the bomb be used against Japan.

"General Marshall said in Potsdam that if the bomb worked we would save a quarter of a million American lives and probably save millions of Japanese.

"I gave careful thought to what my advisers had counseled. I wanted to weigh all the possibilities and implications. Here was the most powerful weapon of destruction ever devised and perhaps it was more than that.

"Conscious of how great a responsibility had been placed on me I suggested to Secretary Stimson that we give Japan a warning in advance by sending Japan an ultimatum to surrender. Some weeks earlier, Stimson had been urging some open declaration or message to the Japanese. I now felt the time was opportune.

"I then asked Stimson to indicate on the map what cities the military would favor as targets, if Japan did not surrender, and we had to use the bomb. Among the targets was Hiroshima, an army center and a military supply port; and Nagasaki, a major seaport containing large industrial establishments.

"I then agreed to the use of the atomic bomb if Japan did not yield.

"I had reached a decision after long and careful thought. It was not an easy decision to make. I did not like the weapon. But I had no qualms if in the long run millions of lives could be saved.

"The rest is history.

"In my statement, released from the White House on August 6, 1945, I said:

" 'The fact that we can release atomic energy ushers in a new era of man's understanding of nature's forces. Atomic energy may in the future supplement the power that now comes from coal, oil and water.'

"This is even more certain today.

"We must harness this great energy source of nature unlocked by man for the benefit and not the destruction of man. Today it helps protect us, tomorrow it will also serve us."

VI

President Truman considers his Point Four Program the most important peace policy development of his administration. He is giving this subject his closest personal attention and deep study. He is in constant and frequent consultation about it with experts on agriculture, industry, finance, labor and public health.

The President says:

"I consider Point Four a practical answer to a growing crisis in a world torn between aggression and peace.

"The Truman Doctrine, the Marshall Plan, the North Atlantic Pact, the mobilization program and the action by the United Nations in meeting the military aggression in Korea were steps dictated by a series of emergencies.

"We have bought time at great expense and a terrible cost of lives and fortune and now we must use that time intelligently and courageously. We face serious trouble unless we realize that our own welfare and that of the rest of the world depend upon the constant and dynamic expansion of the world's resources. The fears that the world is growing too small are groundless. There is room and shelter and food for millions more if we put our know-how to work.

"Point Four takes its name from the fourth position on recommendations to the Congress in my inaugural address in 1949. Point Four is not intended to be a wholesale give-away plan.

"Briefly stated, Point Four is a proposition to take over the gap that is left by the failure of colonialism, only it is different from colonialism in that its objective is to help people to help themselves, with the theory that prosperity of all parts of the world means the prosperity of the whole world.

"We have got to see that the people who occupy the highly congested and populated countries have at least something to eat. And that is not beyond the bounds of possibility. For instance, in Ethiopia there is an area of 65,000 square miles where the soil is as rich as the black soil of northern Illinois, Iowa and Missouri. This soil is capable of supporting and feeding 100 million people. This doesn't mean that the 100 million would actually have to live there but it would provide towards supporting 100 million people elsewhere.

"There are vast areas in other parts of Africa that can be turned into agricultural lands. And in a number of regions in South America there are similar opportunities for expansion of the world's food supply.

"What we want to do under Point Four is to help develop these resources for the benefit of the people who own them.

"Unless we can do these things, we will never have world peace.

"The more people produce and earn around the world, the more we would benefit from it, as they would benefit. It would provide a new market for our huge industrial capacity and an outlet for American capital.

"How do you reckon this country was developed? England and France and Germany and Holland furnished the money for the opening of the west, for the building of the railroads. For instance, Kansas City Southern Railroad was built by Dutch capital. The British developed ranches in Texas and Colorado and all over the southwest, and some of them are still owned by British capital. But that didn't hurt us.

"I have had long talks with Churchill and the French President Auriol and the French statesmen Pleven and Schuman about the Point Four plan of helping people to help themselves around the world, and we can use experts of all nations.

"I have talked to the Presidents of Brazil, Uruguay, Chile, Ecuador, Venezuela and Mexico and urged them to help find some way for the protection of proper investments, not on the basis of colonialism, not even on a guaranteed return basis, but merely that the capital investment ought not to be confiscated where used to develop new resources and areas.

"We must do everything we can to help people everywhere get what they want in the way of modern goods to make their lives easier, and this would keep our industrial plant running to supply them. But they must get a chance to earn something so they can pay for what they buy. We want to help them help themselves and in that way the whole world can prosper."

Afterword

I

This book was not planned. It took shape under extraordinary circumstances during very crowded hours of the President at a time when the person and the office of the President have so compelling an influence on the world. The book—growing out of a series of interviews—was to be a combination of text, pictures and captions descriptive and illustrative of the office and incumbent. It was to have been an intimate but not essentially a revealing book of President Truman and his work. But as the project began to unfold it developed historic proportions and significance.

The President turned over to me his personal diaries and private papers. Almost unknown even to his intimate friends, the diaries and private papers brought sudden revelation of an extraordinary man, a man who knows his history and knows what he thinks and how to say it. There are glimpses behind the international and domestic scenes, dramatically highlighting the untiring efforts of the President to prevent another world war, his serene belief in democracy. The President then turned over to me notes about his life. Never before has a man so high in public life written with such candor and permitted publication while still in office. The stark simplicity of his narrative at times matches the beauty and the most manly style of some of our best writers. The President explained his purpose in this letter to me:

The White House, Washington
October 1, 1951

"Dear Bill:

"I have thought long and hard about making available to you my private notes and papers for publication. As you will judge from reading them, nearly all were intended to remain in my personal files. But I have concluded that for the historical record and a broader comprehension by the public of their thirty-second President and the Presidency I should release some of them to you for publication now.

[251]

"I expect there will be those who will construe this as a political act. You and I know better.

"Bill, I have known you throughout my seven years as President, and during that time I have always found in you the objective reporter and penetrating interviewer.

"Within the bounds of the Nation's security, public interest, and good taste as the only restrictions I would impose, I hand you these private papers with every confidence. With this letter I also give you full authority to publish this material in any manner you deem suitable and useful."

II

I owe a special debt of gratitude to my friend David M. Noyes. I have depended greatly on his inspiring counsel and wise guidance, although I hasten to absolve him from any responsibilities for mistakes of commission or omission in this book.

Many have helped in this book. John Farrar, who is a poet of imagination despite the fact he is a publisher. He is a brilliant organizer and was more than a helpful counsellor. And my thanks are due to Roger W. Straus, Jr., who was quick to see the historic book that was in the making. I wish to acknowledge my indebtedness to Mr. David C. Mearns, Chief of the Manuscript Division of the Library of Congress, author of *The Lincoln Papers* and other historical works, and to William J. Hopkins, Executive Clerk of the White House, and an authority on governmental procedure, for their indispensable aid in reading the galley proofs, but I assume responsibility for any final mistakes of facts that may have shown up. Thanks for help and encouragement are due Margaret Farrar, Margherita Bisconti, Maria Sermolino, and to George Hornby and my brother Henry and my son, William Sermolino Hillman.

Mr. Alfred Wagg wishes to acknowledge his indebtedness to Harry Baudu and Edward K. Armour for technical assistance.

III

President Truman designates himself as the thirty-second President of the United States. Official records show him as the thirty-third President. Independent in his thinking in this matter as in other things, Mr. Truman says:

"I am the thirty-second man to be President. If you count the administrations of Grover Cleveland twice because another President held office between Cleveland's first and second terms, you might try to justify the designation of me as thirty-third President. But then why don't you number all the second terms of other Presidents and the third and fourth terms of President Roosevelt, and where will you be. I am the thirty-second President."

WILLIAM HILLMAN